ISRAEL
AMONG THE NATIONS

INTERNATIONAL THEOLOGICAL COMMENTARY

George A. F. Knight and Fredrick Carlson Holmgren
General Editors

ISRAEL AMONG THE NATIONS

A Commentary on the Books of

Nahum and Obadiah

RICHARD J. COGGINS

and

Esther

S. PAUL RE'EMI

WM. B. EERDMANS PUBL. CO., GRAND RAPIDS

THE HANDSEL PRESS LTD, EDINBURGH

Eerdmans edition 0-8028-0048-3
Handsel edition 0-905312-52-X

Library of Congress Cataloging in Publication Data

Coggins, R. J., 1929-
Israel among the nations.
(International theological commentary)
Bibliography: p.
1. Bible. O.T. Nahum—Commentaries. 2. Bible.
O.T. Obadiah—Commentaries. 3. Bible. O.T. Esther—
Commentaries. I. Re'emi, S. P. II. Title.
III. Series.
BS1625.3.C44 1985   224'.9   85-16201
ISBN 0-8028-0048-3

British Library Cataloguing in Publication Data

Coggins, Richard J.
Israel among the nations: a commentary on the
books of Nahum and Obadiah.
(International theological commentary)
1. Bible. O.T. Minor prophets—Commentaries
I. Title II. Re'emi S. Paul III. Series
224'.9077   BS1560

Scripture quotations are from the Revised Standard Version of the Bible, copyrighted 1946, 1952, © 1971, 1973 by the Division of Christian Education of the National Council of Churches of Christ in the U.S.A., and used by permission.

CONTENTS

ABBREVIATIONS

BHS	Biblia Hebraica Stuttgartensia
Heb.	Hebrew
JB	The Jerusalem Bible
KJV	Authorized or King James Version of the Bible
LXX	Septuagint
mg	marginal note to the text of the RSV
MT	Masoretic Text
NEB	The New English Bible
NT	New Testament
OT	Old Testament
RSV	Revised Standard Version
RV	Revised Version

EDITORS' PREFACE

The Old Testament alive in the Church: this is the goal of the *International Theological Commentary*. Arising out of changing, unsettled times, this Scripture speaks with an authentic voice to our own troubled world. It witnesses to God's ongoing purpose and to his caring presence in the universe without ignoring those experiences of life that cause one to question his existence and love. This commentary series is written by front rank scholars who treasure the life of faith.

Addressed to ministers and Christian educators, the *International Theological Commentary* moves beyond the usual critical-historical approach to the Bible and offers a *theological* interpretation of the Hebrew text. The authors of these volumes, therefore, engaging larger textual units of the biblical writings, assist the reader in the appreciation of the theology underlying the text as well as its place in the thought of the Hebrew Scriptures. But more, since the Bible is the book of the believing community, its text in consequence has acquired ever more meaning through an ongoing interpretation. This growth of interpretation may be found both within the Bible itself and in the continuing scholarship of the Church.

Contributors to the *International Theological Commentary* are Christians — persons who affirm the witness of the New Testament concerning Jesus Christ. For Christians, the Bible is *one* scripture containing the Old and New Testaments. For this reason, a commentary on the Old Testament may not ignore the second part of the canon, namely, the New Testament.

Since its beginning, the Church has recognized a special relationship between the two Testaments. But the precise character of this bond has been difficult to define. Thousands of books and articles have discussed the issue. The diversity of views represented in these publications make us aware that the Church is not of one mind in expressing the "how" of this relationship. The authors of this commentary share a developing consensus that any serious explanation of the Old Testament's relationship to the New will uphold the integrity of the Old Testament. Even though Christianity is rooted in the soil of the Hebrew Scriptures, the biblical interpreter must take care lest he "christianize" these Scriptures.

Authors writing in this commentary will, no doubt, hold varied views concerning *how* the Old Testament relates to the New. No attempt has been made to dictate one viewpoint in this matter. With the whole Church, we are convinced that the relationship between the two Testaments is real and substantial. But we recognize also the diversity of opinions among Christian scholars when they attempt to articulate fully the nature of this relationship.

In addition to the Christian Church, there exists another people for whom the Old Testament is important, namely, the Jewish community. Both Jews and Christians claim the Hebrew Bible as Scripture. Jews believe that the basic teachings of this Scripture point toward, and are developed by, the Talmud, which assumed its present form about A.D. 500. Christians, on the other hand, hold that the Old Testament finds its fulfillment in the New Testament. The Hebrew Bible, therefore, "belongs" to both the Church and the Synagogue.

Recent studies have demonstrated how profoundly early Christianity reflects a Jewish character. This fact is not surprising because the Christian movement arose out of the context of first-century Judaism. Further, Jesus himself was Jewish, as were the first Christians. It is to be expected, therefore, that Jewish and Christian interpretations of the Hebrew Bible will reveal similarities *and* disparities. Such is the case. The authors of the *International Theological Commentary* will refer to the various Jewish traditions that they consider important for an appreciation of the Old Testament text. Such references will enrich our understanding of certain biblical passages and, as an extra gift, offer us insight into the relationship of Judaism to early Christianity.

An important second aspect of the present series is its *international* character. In the past, Western church leaders were considered to be *the* leaders of the Church — at least by those living in the West! The theology and biblical exegesis done by these scholars dominated the thinking of the Church. Most commentaries were produced in the Western world and reflected the life-style, needs, and thoughts of its civilization. But the Christian Church is a worldwide community. People who belong to this universal Church reflect differing thoughts, needs, and lifestyles.

Today the fastest growing churches in the world are to be found, not in the West, but in Africa, Indonesia, South America, Korea, Taiwan, and elsewhere. By the end of this century, Christians in these areas will outnumber those who live in the West. In our age, especially, a commentary on the Bible must transcend the parochialism of Western civilization and be sensitive to issues that are the special problems of persons who live outside of the "Christian" West, issues such as race relations, personal survival and fulfillment, liberation, revolution, famine, tyranny, disease, war, the poor, religion and state. Inspired of God, the authors of the Old Testament knew what life is like on the edge of existence. They addressed themselves to everyday people who often faced more than everyday problems. Refusing to limit God to the "spiritual," they portrayed him as one who heard and knew the cries of people in pain (see Exod. 3:7-8). The contributors to the *International Theological Commentary* are persons who prize the writings of these biblical authors as a word of life to our world today. They read the Hebrew Scriptures in the twin contexts of ancient Israel and our modern day.

The scholars selected as contributors underscore the international aspect of the Commentary. Representing very different geographical, ideological, and ecclesiastical backgrounds, they come from over seventeen countries. Besides scholars from such traditional countries as England, Scotland, France, Italy, Switzerland, Canada, New Zealand, Australia, South Africa, and the United States, contributors from the following places are included: Israel, Indonesia, India, Thailand, Singapore, Taiwan, and countries of Eastern Europe. Such diversity makes for richness of thought. Christian scholars living in Buddhist, Muslim, or Socialist lands may be able to offer the World Church insights into the biblical message — insights to which the scholarship of the West could be blind.

The proclamation of the biblical message is the focal concern of the *International Theological Commentary*. Generally speaking, the authors of these commentaries value the historical-critical studies of past scholars, but they are convinced that these studies by themselves are not enough. The Bible is more than an object of critical study; it is the revelation of God. In the written Word, God has disclosed himself and his will to humankind. Our authors see themselves as servants of the Word which, when rightly received, brings *shalom* to both the individual and the community.

—GEORGE A. F. KNIGHT
—FREDRICK CARLSON HOLMGREN

IN WRATH
REMEMBER
MERCY

A *Commentary on the Book of*
Nahum

RICHARD J. COGGINS

CONTENTS

AUTHOR'S PREFACE

I take this opportunity to express my gratitude to friends and colleagues at Kings College, London, and in the Society for Old Testament Study, whose reactions to earlier studies of these prophets have helped me greatly in forming my own understanding; it is of course not to be expected that they should have removed all errors, whether of thought or of expression. Over and above these general thanks, I wish to express my indebtedness to two individuals in particular. Sr. Mary Reaburn undertook the study of Nahum as part of her Master of Theology degree at the University of London with considerable doubt and even reluctance at first, but came eventually to appreciate the richness of that text; her comments and insights were of great assistance in the preparation of this commentary. Dr. George A. F. Knight has put me triply in his debt: first by asking me to contribute to this series; then by his fortitude when the whole project met a succession of obstacles; and finally by his patience in awaiting a manuscript long after its originally promised date.

London
Richard J. Coggins
May 1984

INTRODUCTION

1. NAHUM AMONG THE PROPHETS

There have characteristically been two main ways for students of the Bible to begin to understand the prophets of ancient Israel. Sometimes the approach has been through the biographical details which are found in some of the prophetic collections. Thus, many studies of Hosea have speculated about the reasons for his marriage, the effects this may have had upon his life and ministry, and the way in which his message reflects the love shown in his relations with Gomer. Jeremiah, too, has often been approached in this personal "psychological" fashion. Alternatively, another favored method has been to isolate some key feature of the prophet's message and to group all the material around that nucleus. Thus we have "Amos the prophet of righteousness," "Hosea the prophet of loving-kindness," and so on.

There has in recent years been much criticism of this kind of approach, and certainly such a way of beginning the study of Nahum would not yield very profitable results. Of Nahum's life we know nothing; his date remains disputed; the first verse of the book mentions his place of origin, but its whereabouts is unknown. At the personal level all that we can say of Nahum is that he must have lived at a time when the Assyrian menace was acute, for it is a theme which runs through much of the book. Nor is it prudent to attempt to categorize Nahum's message within some neat comprehensive slogan. At best we might think of him as the prophet of Yahweh's all-embracing sovereignty over the nations; but such a description is not only clumsy in expression — it also begs many questions and poses many problems. It is wiser not to engage in such a categorization.

All of this means that Nahum has been much neglected. Outline surveys of Israel's prophets usually concentrate on the 8th

cent.—Amos and Hosea, Isaiah and Micah—and then pass on
to the prophets of the last days of the kingdom of Judah—Jeremiah and perhaps Zephaniah—with scarcely any reference to
Nahum. No one will claim that he is the greatest of Israel's
prophets. Yet his words undoubtedly embody a message for us,
and in the light of modern trends in the study of the prophets
the lack of biographical detail or of an easily memorable sum-
mary of his message may not be a disadvantage. Many recent
writers have been very skeptical of the propriety of the "psychological" approach which has so long been popular (see R. P. Carroll, *From Chaos to Covenant*, 5-29). Furthermore, the labeling of
a prophet's message by the use of one simple phrase has always
seemed too easy and has represented a failure to come to terms
with the riches of the tradition underlying each book—riches
both by way of the many layers of additions and developments
through which all prophetic works have passed, riches also in
terms of the differing theological nuances found in each book.
(And what modern preacher or teacher would wish to have his
message summed up in just one phrase?) So perhaps Nahum will
in the future not seem so out of line; perhaps his place among
the prophets can be better evaluated as new methods of study
develop.

Since therefore neither a "psychological" approach nor concentration on one particular theme is likely to prove helpful in
our study of Nahum, we shall be wiser to begin with what is, at
least in principle, a purely objective study: the actual form of the
book as it has come down to us.

2. LITERARY STRUCTURE

Some prophetic collections lend themselves very readily to formal
analysis. For example, Amos, with its repeated and clearly defined series of introductions ("Thus says the LORD"; "Hear this
word"; "Woe to . . ."), leaves little room for dispute as to the
extent and nature of the units which comprise the complete collection. With Nahum, however, the position is much less clear,
and any suggested outline of its structure must be somewhat
tentative. It is instructive to notice that the standard manual of
form criticism, J. H. Hayes, ed., *OT Form Criticism*, contains in
its biblical index no reference at all to Nahum. We shall see in

the Commentary that it is impossible to divide Nahum's message into neat and self-contained segments. It is only with these provisoes and cautions, therefore, that the following outline structure may be proposed.

1:1	Title
1:2-8	Hymn in acrostic form, proclaiming the might of Yahweh
1:9-11	Accusations against the community, in question form
1:12-15	Oracles containing words both of promise and of condemnation
2:1-2	Transition from warnings against Judah to the Nineveh poems
2:3-12	Poems proclaiming the defeat of an enemy army, now applied to Nineveh
2:13	Prose oracle; an announcement of judgment, now applied to Nineveh
3:1-19	"Woe" (i.e., funeral dirge) against Nineveh (Though the section is not homogeneous, in its present form it has been drawn together to express a single theme.)

Even from so brief an outline, it is possible to sense something of the difficulty in establishing with confidence the literary form of the book. That there is no general agreement on formal matters may be illustrated by the fact that one recent proposal regards the book as "a letter written in exile in order to encourage the depressed branch of the LORD's people still dwelling in the promised land" (A. S. van der Woude, "The Book of Nahum: A Letter Written in Exile," *Oudtestamentische Studiën* 20 [1977]: 124). Such a view seems to raise as many new problems as it solves and will not be discussed further here, but it well illustrates the uncertainties with regard to formal structure.

Nevertheless, the overall thematic thrust is clear enough: the absolute sovereignty of Yahweh is proclaimed. That theme is applied, partly as a warning against the prophet's own community, but to a far greater extent against Nineveh, seen as symbolizing the Assyrian Empire, which exercised dominion over Judah for the greater part of a century. Throughout the book we shall find that literary allusions greatly outnumber historical references. Of the latter, the only one which can be established with confidence is that to the sack of Thebes in 663 B.C. (Nah. 3:8-10). This is a sufficient indication to place the activity of Nahum in the 7th cent., but it may be somewhat misleading to describe it as a genuinely historical reference. Though there is no good reason for doubting that the original inspiration for these verses was the destruction of Thebes, the actual allusion says little of the event itself. Rather, it is couched in the standard imagery of such accounts, and thus in its own way provides additional evidence for the predominance of literary allusions in the book of Nahum.

Many allusions of this kind will be noted and discussed in the Commentary, but at this point two introductory comments should be made. First, we need to remind ourselves of the very severe limits of our knowledge of the actual circumstances of prophetic "inspiration" (using that much-abused term here in the sense of "the prompting . . . of the utterance or publication of particular views"; *Shorter Oxford English Dictionary, ad loc.*). In other words, why did prophetic oracles take the particular form that they did? There are too many similarities between oracles attributed to different prophets to allow us realistically to suppose that each prophetic word is simply the result of direct divine "inspiration" (to use the word now in its more familiar sense). Clearly, there were certain accepted models: figures of speech, modes of expression, and the like, which went some way toward determining the particular form in which an individual prophet's message would be couched. For this reason it is not necessary when very similar oracles occur in two different prophetic collections that there should have been a literary dependence of one upon the other. Each may have been drawing upon an established stock of oracular material and adopting it for its own purpose.

A classic example of this in the book of Nahum occurs at 1:15, where we find words strongly reminiscent of Isa. 52:7. It is characteristic of the neglect of Nahum that these words have often been discussed in their Isaianic context, of the hoped-for deliverance of Jerusalem from Babylonian control, but rarely treated in their context in Nahum. We shall see other examples of similarities between Nahum and Isa. 40–55 (and indeed other prophetic collections); it would be wrong to suppose that the most likely reason for such linkages is literary dependence in either direction.

3. Nahum as a Cult Prophet

The second introductory comment with regard to literary forms in Nahum can also be introduced from this same verse (Nah. 1:15), the second half of which differs from the passage in Isaiah.

> *Keep your feasts, O Judah,*
> *fulfil your vows.*

This allusion to the cultic round in Judah (and here we must assume that the reference is to the temple in Jerusalem) raises the question whether Nahum was himself in some way involved in an official capacity in the Jerusalem cult.

There are two separate problems here. The first concerns the specific link to Jerusalem; the second is the more general question of "cult prophets." On the first point, it is right to note that, as A. S. van der Woude has pointed out, "Nahum does not show any special interest in Jerusalem. He neither mentions the city nor alludes to it. . . . There is no allusion at all to election, covenant, or Jerusalem and Zion" ("The Book of Nahum," 120). While van der Woude's further conclusion that Nahum was one of the northern exiles may seem doubtful, it is certainly important to bear in mind that links with other prophetic collections are of a literary kind only. Our ignorance about the life and circumstances of the individual character Nahum remains almost complete.

With regard to "cult prophets" there has been much discussion in recent years, but not always the degree of clarity that might be hoped for. Sometimes "cult prophet" has been little more than a term of abuse: the true prophet was the free preacher attacking the corrupt practices of the cult, and therefore any prophet involved in the cult must be at least suspect. That there are attacks upon the cult in many prophetic collections is clear enough (Isa. 1:10-17; Hos. 6:6; Amos 5:21-24 are among the most familiar examples). But it is now very widely agreed that it would be wrong to universalize these condemnations and to deduce from them that true prophets were necessarily opposed to the cult. Both the use of cultic forms in prophetic books and the incorporation of "prophetic"-type passages in various Psalms suggest that the relation between prophecy and cult is a more complex

9

one than has often been proposed. John H. Eaton suggests that the book of Nahum is to be understood within a context of festal rites, probably those of the Jerusalem autumn festival (*Vision in Worship*, 14-21); while an attractive proposal, it cannot be established with complete confidence.

For our present purpose, rather, it is right to recognize that the literary usage of Nahum may often imply an indebtedness to the language of the cult. It would be unwise to go further than that, both because of the relative lack of terms in the book which are clearly "Jerusalemite" and because of the paucity of our assured knowledge of the Jerusalem cult. In this last connection it is relevant to note that the two important studies by A. R. Johnson relating to cultic prophets (*The Cultic Prophet in Ancient Israel* and *The Cultic Prophet and Israel's Psalmody*), valuable though they are, have more to say about that material in the Psalms which shows analogies with prophetic oracles than about the role of the prophets themselves. In sum, then, we may say that a good deal of the material in the book shows affinities with what appears to be "cultic usage" (I interpret this phrase more fully in "An Alternative Prophetic Tradition?" in *Israel's Prophetic Tradition*, 91-92). We have no means of deciding whether or not it is proper to go further and claim some kind of cultic status for Nahum himself. As stated at the outset, of Nahum as an individual we must recognize our ignorance.

4. THEOLOGY

The books of Deuteronomy and Jeremiah, both roughly contemporary with Nahum, show great concern with the problem of false prophecy. Jeremiah 23:9-40 contains oracles denouncing the false prophets of his time, and ch. 28 gives a graphic description of Jeremiah's confrontation with Hananiah. The exposition of the prophetic role in Deut. 13:1-5 and 18:15-22 expresses similar concerns. There is no clear agreement, either in the biblical passages or among their modern interpreters, as to the precise nature of this "falsity"; but one theme that emerges, especially in Jer. 28, is that the true prophet "prophesied war, famine, and pestilence" (v. 8), whereas the prophet whose message is one of peace should be treated with suspicion (v. 9).

The usual fate of Nahum in assessments of the theology of the prophets has been to be ignored completely. Sometimes, however, a more specifically negative verdict has been reached, and the prophet has been regarded as, or at least compared with, one of the false prophets opposed in Deuteronomy and Jeremiah. Thus J. M. Powis Smith, in the *International Critical Commentary* more than seventy years ago, asserted that Nahum's stance is "essentially one with that of such men as Hananiah" and is "a representative of the old, narrow and shallow prophetism" (Smith, Ward, and Bewer, *Micah, etc.,* 281). In fact, of course, he does not fit at all into the pattern of warnings laid down by Jeremiah, for his message was certainly not one of peace. Where he does differ from the majority of the prophets whose oracles have been preserved in the canonical books is in the fact that — at least in its present form — most of Nahum is directed against Israel's enemies rather than against Israel or Judah. (The cautionary phrase "at least in its present form" is necessary, because the attempt has been made, notably by Jörg Jeremias, to show that Nahum's words of doom were originally directed against his own people *[Kultprophetie und Gerichtsverkündigung in der späten Königszeit Israels]*. That standpoint has not been widely accepted, but it does draw our attention to the fact that much of the language in the book was of a type that could be used and reused against different groups.)

If it be accepted that Nahum's oracles are addressed to Israel's enemies, clearly there are ample parallels for this. A characteristic feature of the major prophetic collections is what are commonly called "oracles against foreign nations." Isaiah 13–23, Jer. 46–51, Ezek. 25–32, and Amos 1–2 are the most familiar examples of the genre. It is customary to describe such collections as "oracles against foreign nations," but such a description can be somewhat misleading. Whatever may have been the origin of this particular form (and the question remains in dispute), the tendency increasingly was for oracles of this type to move away from concern with the empirical state of affairs in a particular nation toward an emphasis on asserting Yahweh's power over all other gods and their devotees. Such a development is especially characteristic of the exilic period; and it seems proper to regard it as the main theological thrust of Nahum. By the time that the book reached its final form, Assyria would have become a typical rather than an actual enemy, standing for all who dared to oppose Yahweh and those whom he employed for his purposes. Language from a cultic and possibly a mythical background could be employed to show how the victory and salvation there proclaimed had been actualized in the overthrow of Assyria.

In many ways it is proper to draw a comparison between Nahum and Isa. 40–55. Already we have seen one example of literary association, and there are other, less specific links which will be discussed in the Commentary. There is also a similarity in theology, in that each prophet is concerned to show the sovereignty of Yahweh, at a time when to all earthly appearances both he and his people had been reduced to utter powerlessness.

In this connection it may be significant to note the position which Nahum occupies in the final form of the OT. For the most part, we are so concerned with examining each prophetic "book" as an individual unit that we ignore the fact that the minor prophets in particular also comprise a "book" collectively: the Book of the Twelve. In that book Nahum has particular links with Jonah, next to which it is placed in some manuscripts of the Minor Prophets, especially in the LXX (H. B. Swete, *An Introduction to the OT in Greek*, 201-2). Such an association may be traced back at least as far as the earliest manuscripts of the apocryphal book Tobit. At Tob. 14:4 some manuscripts, followed by the RV and RSV, speak of *Jonah's* prediction of Nineveh's overthrow, while others, followed by JB and NEB, mention *Nahum* at this point. This is not the place to discuss which reading in the book of Tobit is more satisfactory, but the association of the two prophets is easy to understand. Each explores the theme of Assyria, symbolized by its capital, Nineveh, as the typical enemy—an enemy which inspires dread in the worshipers of Yahweh. The two prophetic recollections illustrate two possible fates for such enemies: if they persist in their self-confident arrogance, destruction is inevitable (Nahum); but it might be that in the providence of Yahweh even the deadliest enemies could repent and be accepted, and if that were to be so would Israel be willing to accept such repentance (Jonah)? In this respect it is noteworthy that Nahum and Jonah are the only two books in the whole Bible which end with a question (cf. T. F. Glasson, "The Final Question in Nahum and Jonah," *Expository Times* 81 [1969]: 54-55). To such questions the books themselves supply in important measure their own answer, in the depiction of

Yahweh found in strikingly similar terms in each book; the origin of the phraseology may be cultic, but its present thrust is clearly theological. So in Jonah we find: "Thou art a gracious God and merciful, slow to anger, and abounding in steadfast love, and repentest of evil" (Jonah 4:2); in Nahum, "The LORD is slow to anger and of great might, and the LORD will by no means clear the guilty" (Nah. 1:3). (The similarity would be even greater if, with BHS and some commentators, we were to read *hesed* instead of *koah* in the Nahum passage: "great in steadfast love" instead of "of great might"; but such an emendation seems unnecessary.)

Whatever be made of this particular linkage, the basic point surely remains valid, that the foreign nations oracles came increasingly to be used as a vehicle for asserting the sovereignty of Yahweh. By the end of the OT period, the nations are scarcely traceable as such; they have become symbols of all that is opposed to the supreme power of Israel's God. Nahum marks an important point in the development in this direction. The foreign enemy against whom he inveighs is recognizably Assyria, an all too real empirical threat to Judah's peace of mind at the time of the prophet's ministry. Yet the real center of gravity is not in Nineveh; the real concern is with Yahweh's power, and to that extent Nineveh symbolizes all that might stand in opposition to that power.

To a great degree Nahum is a "one-theme" prophet. The collected oracles of the 8th-cent. prophets (assuming that they in some measure accurately reflect the range of concerns of those after whom they are now named) show them to have been involved with a whole spectrum of issues. There were for them many ways in which the community of their day had failed to measure up to the obligations laid upon them. On the other hand, it is increasingly the case in the later parts of the collection of the Minor Prophets that the interest is focused upon one overarching concern, even if that concern might be expressed in a variety of ways. We shall see this to be true of Obadiah in the later part of this volume, and it is certainly so with Nahum. He proclaims the sovereignty of Yahweh, a sovereignty which was still effective even when his people were under the control of a brutal foreign enemy; but it could be seen even more clearly when that enemy was receiving its just deserts. At times, as will become apparent in the Commentary, the precise way in which that basic

13

conviction is expressed is not entirely clear; but there can be no doubt of the centrality and depth of it.

5. LATER INTERPRETATION

Reference has already been made to the way in which Nahum is often neglected in contemporary study of the prophets. This neglect is not a purely modern phenomenon. Of two possible allusions to Nahum in the NT, one (Rom. 10:15) is much more likely to be based on Isa. 52:7, with which, as we have noted, Nahum is virtually identical. The second, the description of the whore of Babylon (Rev. 17:2), may include Nah. 3:4 among the passages which contributed to its final form. Sexual imagery of this kind in polemic descriptions is, however, too common to allow us to posit any direct dependence.

It had long seemed as if a similar neglect was characteristic of the Jewish writings of the intertestamental period, with the reference in Tob. 14:4 as a doubtful exception. The discovery of the Dead Sea Scrolls has, however, led to a significant modification of this view. The Scrolls formed a part (how substantial a part, we have no means of knowing) of the library of the Qumran community, whom most modern scholars have identified with the Essenes. That library contained not only biblical texts, amongst which fragments of Nahum are to be included, but also commentaries on those texts, including one, again in fragmentary condition, on Nahum (4QpNah). It is characteristic of these commentaries to apply the words of the prophet to the life-situation of the community; but whereas that is normally done in a veiled and allusive fashion, the Nahum Commentary is remarkable in that it specifies by name those contemporary rulers whom it regards as the "real" concerns of the passage being discussed.

The Dead Sea fragment which has survived is Nah. 2:11-13, a passage describing the ravages of lions, the reference of which is by no means clear in the biblical text. The Qumran commentary applies it to two 2nd-cent. rulers of Antioch, described in the commentary as "kings of Greece," for they were among the successors of Alexander the Great. They are Demetrius and Antiochus. Though Antiochus is mentioned second, it appears from the context as if he were the earlier of the two rulers. It is virtually certain that the reference here is to Antiochus IV Epiphanes

(175-163), whose attacks upon the Jews are described in 1 Maccabees and alluded to in Daniel (for a translation of the fragment see G. Vermes, *The Dead Sea Scrolls in English*, 231-32). Demetrius is less certainly identifiable, but it is most probable that this was Demetrius III, who died in 88 B.C. For our present concerns, however, precise identifications are not important. More important than the often obscure details of the history of the 2nd and 1st cents. B.C. is the fact that by that period the prophet's words had come to be understood as being addressed to a situation far removed from his own day. That is to say, they had come to be regarded as "prophetic" in the popular sense of the term, as applying to a far distant future. Throughout our Commentary we shall need to bear in mind both the attempt to understand the words of the book in their original setting and the way in which they have been interpreted as "sacred writings" in religious communities through the ages.

One other reference to ancient understanding of Nahum may be made, since it too offers some suggestion that the book was not so neglected as might at first sight appear. The Jewish historian Flavius Josephus, writing in the 1st cent. A.D., when describing events in the 8th cent. B.C. dates Nahum (wrongly) in that period and then proceeds, most unusually, to quote a section from the book verbatim. By a curious coincidence the passage quoted, Nah. 2:8-13, is substantially identical with the passage found in the Qumran fragment and is the only such extended quotation from the OT to be found in Josephus. Since Josephus asserts that Nahum's prophecy came true with the downfall of Nineveh, dated by the historian 115 years later, he also clearly understood Nahum as a prophet speaking of events which would take place in the distant future (*Antiquities* ix.11.3).

CHAPTER 1

1 This introductory verse clearly serves as a title, but, as is still sometimes the case today, it is probable that the "author" did not choose his own title. Rather, this usage reflects the perception of a later generation as to the contents of these chapters. For that reason, since this verse can in a sense be regarded as the oldest interpretation known to us of the words of Nahum, it is worth studying in some detail.

The Nahum collection is here described as a *massa*. Older English versions, such as the RV, rendered this Hebrew term as "burden," in accordance with its most natural etymological derivation; but the usual modern translation is "oracle," as in the RSV. In one sense that is undoubtedly right, for the prevalence of the word as an introduction to prophetic collections — either whole books (Habakkuk, Malachi) or smaller units within books (Isa. 13:1 and frequently elsewhere in Isaiah; Zech. 9:1; 12:1) — shows that the word had a technical sense within the circles that gathered together prophetic oracles. As such it seems characteristically to be associated with Jerusalem and the southern kingdom of Judah. But it is perhaps wrong to ignore the etymological aspect altogether, for there are other passages where the sense of "burden" is clearly present. Some of these suggest a deliberate link between the theme of prophetic words of judgment and that of a heavy load needing to be carried. Jeremiah 23:33-40 provides an elaborate wordplay whose exact sense is difficult to capture, but it clearly depends upon these two related senses of *massa*. It seems likely, therefore, that the neutral term "oracle" here does not convey the whole sense; there is also an implicit idea of "judgment."

The theme of this *massa* is expressed: "concerning Nineveh." Here it is important to remember that this was the title applied by the final editor of the collection. Some of Nahum's oracles were certainly addressed to Nineveh, but that may not necessarily be true of all of them. We have already seen (Introduction, pp. 6-8) that the Nineveh poems actually occupy chs. 2 – 3 of the book, and it is not beyond dispute whether all of these poems were originally concerned with Nineveh. It may be appropriate here to see two stages of a process. First, poems speaking in general terms of the defeat of an enemy army and of the inevitability of judgment have been applied to the Assyrian threat in a specific way and understood as such in chs. 2 – 3 of the book. Second, at a later stage the whole book has been interpreted as being addressed to Nineveh.

The site of ancient Nineveh has been thoroughly explored. It is situated in what is now Iraq, near Mosul. Ever since the work of Austen Henry Layard in the mid-19th cent., Western archaeologists have been active in investigating the site, and their efforts have more recently been supplemented by the work of Iraqi scholars. (For a survey of the evidence, see D. J. Wiseman, "Nineveh," *The Illustrated Bible Dictionary* 2: 1089-92.)

But excessive concentration on archaeological discoveries can have its dangers. It is likely that already in the time of Nahum Nineveh had become a symbol, standing for the heathen enemy of God and his people. Such a development is obvious enough in the book of Jonah, and still more so, of course, in the only NT use of the term (Matt. 12:41 = Luke 11:30). It may also be detected in the passage in Zephaniah, approximately contemporary with Nahum and strongly reminiscent of it in tone:

> *[The LORD] will stretch out his hand against the north, and destroy Assyria;*
> *and he will make Nineveh a desolation, a dry waste like the desert.*
> *(Zeph. 2:13)*

The point relating to symbolic use is an important one for the modern reader of Nahum and other OT prophets: historical and archaeological knowledge is fascinating and instructive, but it is not the only criterion by which to judge prophetic words. Nineveh was not only the capital of the Assyrian Empire; it was also a symbol of the forces of evil, and as such it was a symbol which could legitimately be reapplied to new situations. Thus the NT can call the Rome of its day Babylon, as at Rev. 18:2.

The collection is called a *sepher* (RSV "book," more accurately
a scroll). No other prophetic collection is so described in its introduction, but among the prophets of the 7th and 6th cents.
references to scrolls are frequent: Jeremiah's words were written
down on a *sepher* (Jer. 36:2), and for both Habakkuk and Ezekiel
the theme of a scroll (Heb. *megillah*) is important (Hab. 2:2; Ezek.
3). Though this introductory verse, referring as it does to Nahum
in the third person, is from a date later than the actual delivery
of the oracles, we need not assume a long delay.

Nahum's words are described as a "vision." Again there are
close links with other prophetic collections, and again the usage
appears to be characteristically Jerusalemite. These links go beyond what we should naturally regard as ocular experiences, such
as Isaiah's vision in the temple (Isa. 6). Several prophetic collections are introduced as "visions" (Isa. 1:1; Amos 1:1, literally,
"the words which he saw"; Obad. 1; Hab. 1:1, "the *massa* which
he saw"). Clearly the characteristic modern Western distinction
between speaking and seeing, regarding them as two different
"senses," is irrelevant here. Perhaps we may realize more fully
what the usage implies if we call to mind the modern use of such
words as "insight" or the common expression "I see what you
mean."

The prophet himself is called "Nahum of Elkosh." Elkosh is
presumably a place name, though its location is unknown. Various suggestions have been made: in Galilee; near Nineveh; in
the Shephelah, west of Judah (the most frequent identification).
In fact none of these is more than guesswork. As to Nahum's
own name, it is formed from the common Hebrew root meaning
"comfort, console," but it is difficult from the content of his oracles to see any special significance in his name. It is effectively
the same as the name Nehemiah, with the theophorous element
(compounding it with the divine name Yahweh) lacking.

2-8 These verses present a feature which is almost impossible
to reproduce without great artificiality in most modern Western
languages. They are part of an acrostic, a poem each of whose
astrophes begins with a succeeding letter of the Hebrew alphabet,
which has twenty-two letters. There are many examples in the
Hebrew Bible, notably in the Psalms and the book of Lamentations, of the acrostic pattern being carried through the complete

alphabet. Some earlier scholars attempted to emend the text so as to obtain such a complete acrostic here. The influence of their efforts can still be detected in the NEB, which contains the footnote, "Verses 2-14 are an incomplete alphabetic acrostic poem; some parts have been re-arranged accordingly" (details of the emendations are set out in L. H. Brockington, *The Hebrew Text of the OT*, 257-58). In fact it is only by dint of drastic surgery upon the text that anything approaching a complete acrostic can be reconstructed. Although some scholars still attempt to include vv. 9-10 in the acrostic pattern — which is thereby extended to something like fifteen letters of the alphabet — it seems more likely that the acrostic is confined to vv. 2-8. If so, this would involve eleven letters, the first half of the alphabet. It remains open to question whether this proportion is significant; it has been suggested that "if an entire acrostic conveys completeness, half an acrostic may well be a prophetic way of indicating completeness with still more to come" (D. L. Christensen, *Transformations of the War Oracle in OT Prophecy*, 171). Not all will find this argument convincing. It is probably better to admit freely that we do not know the circumstances which led to this poem being left in this apparently incomplete state, either by Nahum himself or by the redactors of the material. Certainly at some point the very existence of an acrostic seems to have become obscured, for even to achieve the eleven-line pattern requires some minor textual adjustment.

More important than what must inevitably be vain speculation about the original extent of this poem is the fact that the other suviving examples of the genre, in Psalms and Lamentations, all appear to have been related to the Jerusalem cult. Whether they functioned in a particular and specific way, we do not know; the traditional theory is that they served a pedagogical or mnemonic purpose. However that may be, it is clear that we have in this poem one of the many indications of a close link between Nahum and the cultic usage of his day. We should perhaps be wary of labeling Nahum as a "cultic prophet" (see above, pp. 9-10), but it is nevertheless true that we see here the first example of a phenomenon which will recur throughout the book — that is, a close relation to and a willingness to adopt cultic forms. In our more detailed analysis of this poem it will not be surprising

19

if some of the closest parallels to Nahum's usage are to be found in the Psalms.

2   We have no account of Nahum's call to be a prophet, but this verse supplies one of the important functions of the prophetic call accounts: to assert the nature of the God who is doing the calling. (Isaiah 6 and Ezek. 1, though in very different styles, are the most obvious examples of complete call narratives.) Here the particular emphasis is that Yahweh is "jealous" and "avenging." In English both these words have a profoundly negative character, and they well illustrate the difficulty in translation, for that negative sense is not implicit in the Hebrew. Both words are indeed strongly positive. Hebrew *qanno*, the word translated as "jealous," is best known for its occurrence (in a slightly different form) in the Ten Commandments (Exod. 20:5); there it is found in what is probably a late elaboration of the commandment against making and serving graven images. The point it emphasizes is the supremacy and incomparability of Yahweh, the God of Israel, who is the true God. "Let God be God." As Brevard S. Childs has rightly noted when commenting on the passage in the Decalogue: "In the Old Testament Yahweh's zeal [jealousy] is very closely related to his holiness" (*The Book of Exodus*, 405).

The second word, *noqem* ("avenging"), is emphasized by its use three times in this verse. (The RSV introduces variety, which is needed in English translation, by rendering the last use "takes vengeance," but the Hebrew is identical in all three phrases.) The "tit-for-tat" associations which spring to mind with English words such as "vengeance" or "avenging" are not present here. Rather, the connotations are juridical. Instead of unlimited violence being unleashed when an injury is suffered, "vengeance" means that justice will be done by the appropriate amount of compensation being awarded or by punishment inflicted, *and no more*. God's holiness and his justice are emphasized by these two unpromising sounding words. This, then, is a twin theme which runs through much of Nahum.

These assertions of Yahweh's character imply that there is injustice in the world which needs to be put right; and such injustice implies anger. The OT does not hesitate to associate anger with God; indeed, divine wrath is spoken of in no fewer than eighty-five passages with this particular word, *hemah* (RSV

"wrathful"). Such anger will, of course, regularly be characterized as directed against "his adversaries"; but that expression
may include not only Israel's enemies but also, in the frequent
times of its falling-away, Israel itself.

One striking feature of the Hebrew text of this verse seems to
be ignored by virtually all English translations. The three phrases
which make up its first half are, literally rendered, "jealous El,
avenging Yahweh, angry Baal." That is to say, the two great
Canaanite deities, El and Baal, are used as alternative designations of Yahweh. The identification with El is not unusual in the
Old Testament; links with Baal are much less frequent, since
most references to Baal are hostile. It is, however, the Deuter-
onomic literature which is particularly opposed to Baal; elsewhere there are clear signs that Baal and Yahweh were not
regarded as totally irreconcilable (for example, one son of David
is given a name compounded with Baal, "Beeliada" [1 Chron.
14:7], whereas at least one other son, Adonijah, bore a name
compounded with Yahweh). It should also be recognized that the
word *baal* in Hebrew means simply "master" or "lord," so that
the phrase here, *baal hemah*, represents a Hebrew idiom which is
perfectly properly translated "wrathful," as in the RSV. Nevertheless it remains true that the juxtaposition of these three divine
names in one line of poetry is surely a deliberate dramatic device.

3 This verse falls into two clearly defined halves, which need
to be considered separately. The first half is a formula found in
substantially similar form elsewhere in the OT. It has been omitted from the present context by some translations (e.g., NEB) as
being nothing more than a later copyist's gloss. The difficulty
with such an approach is that the main argument in its support
is dangerously double-edged. If, as is argued, the sentiments of
this formula are out of line with those found generally in Nahum,
why should a glossator have inserted them? In fact this half-verse
may legitimately be seen as balancing the picture of Yahweh's
nature provided by v. 2. Though it is still emphasized that God
"will by no means clear the guilty" (*yenaqqeh*, here translated
"clear," seems to be a deliberate wordplay with *noqem* "avenging"
in the previous verse), that is not the only aspect of his nature.
He is also "slow to anger and of great might." This phrase is

very similar to the description of Yahweh's self-revelation found in Exod. 34:6-7 (where the identical warning that he "will by no means clear the guilty" is also found), and in Ps. 145:8. (We have already seen that a very similar divine designation is found in Jonah 4:2; see above, p. 13.) The significance of the phrase in its present context for our understanding is twofold. First, its probable liturgical usage suggests a link between Nahum and the cult of a type of which we shall see further evidence as we proceed. Second, it brings out the double aspect of Yahweh's character as it was revealed to his prophet. God was both the one whose anger and strict demand for justice meant certain trouble for those who resisted his will and the one who would respond eagerly and willingly to any sign of change among mankind. It has been shown by Robert C. Dentan that this particular expression of belief in Yahweh was especially characteristic of the period from the 7th cent. onward ("The Literary Affinities of Exodus XXXIV 6f," *Vetus Testamentum* 13 [1963]: 34-51). Dentan cites no fewer than nine passages where the phrase is used as a whole or in part, and seven others where it is echoed. Thus we find evidence here of the links between Nahum and the main Yahwistic tradition of his time. The minor variations with which the formula is quoted render unnecessary here the emendation of *koah* ("might") to *hesed* ("loving-kindness"), proposed by some earlier commentators and still suggested as possible in BHS.

In the second half of v. 3 the acrostic is resumed with a vivid description of a theophany. God's awe-inspiring presence is evoked in language reminiscent of the Psalms (cf. Ps. 18:7-15) and of Isaiah (Isa. 29:6), and perhaps also recalling the divine presence in the cloud in the account of the Exodus.

4 Probably the first half of this verse should be taken with what precedes, as part of the account of the theophany. It is characteristic of the whole Bible to be deeply suspicious of the sea; thus, in the Revelation to John part of the promise was that there should be no more sea (Rev. 21:1). To what extent this was due to the empirical fact that Israel never became any kind of maritime power and, like many landlocked nations, always remained somewhat afraid of the unpredictable sea and to what extent we may legitimately trace mythical themes in which the sea is the cosmic deep, always threatening to destroy God-created order, is a matter which is likely to continue to defy certain agreement. One slight pointer toward the second as the more likely explanation may be found in the use of the verb *ga'ar* ("rebuke"), which is most commonly used of God's assertion of his sovereignty over those who try to assert their claims against him (Isa. 17:13; Ps. 68:30); the one occasion when it is used with "sea" as object (Ps. 106:9) is ambiguous in the same way the present verse is. In any case, "the sea" and "the rivers" (is there a reminiscence here of the rivers in the second creation story, Gen. 2:10-14?) are kept firmly under divine control. As elsewhere in Nahum, the closest thematic link is found in Isaiah; Isa. 50:2 differs in form from this passage, being a divine speech, but is virtually identical in theme.

The remainder of this verse, while still descriptive of the theophany, seems more specifically to link the theophany with the theme of Yahweh's battle against the forces of chaos (see S. J. DeVries, "The Acrostic of Nahum in the Jerusalem Liturgy," *Vetus Testamentum* 16 [1966]: 476-81). The first word in the Hebrew text, *umlal* ("wither"), is emended by many commentators since it does not correspond with the acrostic structure which would have us expect a word beginning with the fourth letter of the Hebrew alphabet. Hebrew *umlal* is, in fact, repeated at the end of the verse, and this could be taken to suggest that some corruption has taken place. There is, however, a further complicating factor: this verse shares many details of vocabulary and theme with Isa. 33:9, and it is not self-evident that any improvement is achieved through emendation. If a correction is needed here, the most likely suggestion is perhaps *dalelu* ("are made small," so BHS), which is similar in sound to *umlal*, but this can remain only a speculative reconstruction.

With the references to "Bashan and Carmel" we are again in a realm of language familiar from the Psalms. "Bashan" in Ps. 68:15-16 symbolizes the rebellious forces ranged against Yahweh on Mt. Zion,

> *the mount which God desired for his abode,*
> *yea, where the LORD will dwell for ever.*

"Carmel" is not found in the Psalms, but Amos 1:2 provides a very similar image of the contrast between Mt. Zion, from which

Yahweh "roars," and Carmel, whose summit "withers" — the same idea, though not the same Hebrew word, as is found here. The use of "Lebanon" in the Psalms most frequently symbolizes fertility because of the height and splendor of its native cedars, but in Ps. 29:5-6 we find the same theme that is expressed here, of Lebanon as the rival mountain overwhelmed by "the voice of the LORD."

An even more remarkable parallel with this verse can be found in Isa. 33:9. Not only is Lebanon described as "withering away" (*umlelah*, the same verb that is used here), but Bashan and Carmel are also mentioned. There is no agreement among commentators as to the context of Isa. 33, but it is at least clear that the general picture is of the rout of all of Yahweh's enemies, real or potential, in the face of the overwhelming splendor of the divine presence.

5 These specific examples now give rise to an extended picture of the whole created order struck with terror before the awesome presence of God in the theophany. The most widely found form of this imagery speaks of the earth as quaking, and this language is common to a number of prophetic passages (e.g., Jer. 4:23-28) and Psalms (e.g., Ps. 46:3). Here "the earth" is spoken of as being "laid waste," varying the imagery somewhat, but the overall impression is not significantly altered. All the order imposed at creation is now at risk, and there is the threat of a return to chaos. More than twenty OT passages have been identified in which this is the overall theme, and it seems likely that such a description of the divine presence was a regular feature of the cultic language of Jerusalem. "The hills melt" is expressive of the same devastating picture; interestingly, the closest parallel to this phrase is found in Amos 9:13, as part of a picture of the hopeful future after present evils have passed. (This similarity is not apparent from the RSV, which in Amos has "the hills shall flow," but in each case the same verb, *mug*, is used in the same hithpolel form.)

The RSV translates the next phrase "the earth is laid waste"; though there is no marginal note, this is presumably dependent upon emending MT *tissa* to *tishsha*, from the root *shaah* ("to be ruined"). If the Hebrew text is retained, the sense would be that "the earth lifts up (its voice)," that is, in distress. Whichever text is read, the general sense is clear: the picture of desolation ex-

tends from specific places, through all the main natural features,
to embrace the world itself and its inhabitants.

6 Another literary device frequently found in the descriptions
of a theophany is now introduced: the rhetorical question, with
the implied answer "No one." Here the description of the divine
power is likened to fire, as is also the case in a comparable passage made familiar to many by its use in Handel's *Messiah*,
Mal. 3:2.

> *"Who can endure the day of his coming,*
> *and who can stand when he appears?*
> *For he is like a refiner's fire."*

It is clear that no hesitation was felt in asserting that God's power
could be used for destructive as well as for creative purposes.
Another very instructive comparison with the present passage
can be found in Jer. 4:26, which uses very similar imagery to
speak of God's anger.

> *I looked, and lo, the fruitful land was a desert,*
> *and all its cities were laid in ruins*
> *before the LORD, before his fierce anger.*

The verse ends, not with any formal refrain, but with language
that recalls the imagery of vv. 3b-4.

7 How surprising it is, therefore, to find the assertion, "The
LORD is good." Little in the preceding stanzas has led us to
expect such a development. A partial explanation of this may be
provided by the acrostic form. Not only is such a form not easily
compatible with precise development of thought, but the evidence
of acrostics in the Psalms does seem to suggest that there was
something of a convention that the ninth letter, *tet*, might be used
for an assertion of God's goodness. In the very elaborate acrostic
Ps. 119, for example, in which eight successive verses each begin
with the same initial letter, no fewer than five of the *tet* verses
(vv. 65-72) begin with some form of the root *tob* ("good"). But
the poet whom we are studying is certainly no slave to convention, and a fuller explanation of the apparently abrupt transfor-

mation at this point may lie in the fact that the theophany, here and elsewhere in the OT, is a means by which the true servants of Yahweh are distinguished from those who have rejected him or whom he has rejected.

The links with the Psalms do, however, remain important. In the Psalms the cry "the LORD is good" occurs so frequently that it must surely have been more than a spontaneous burst of praise from the worshipers; it would have been a specific part of the Jerusalem liturgy. Characteristically in the Psalms a reason is then given, and so it is here; even in the terrors of the theophany, the LORD is "a stronghold" for "those who take refuge in him." Psalm 46, in which God is described as a "refuge and strength" (the last word being cognate with that translated "stronghold" here), could properly be read as an extended reflection upon the theme of this verse and the next: God's protection of those who trust in him, and the inevitability of judgment against his adversaries.

8 The acrostic ends with the assertion of that judgment. In words reminiscent of Isa. 28:18 (RSV "overwhelming" and "passes through" are in effect identical with terms here translated "flood" and "overflowing") the certainty of complete and final judgment is asserted. The RSV translation "his adversaries" represents an emendation of the Hebrew, the natural meaning of which would be "her place." The Hebrew text could be retained if the word "place" is given the sense "holy place," which it often has; the reference would then be to the overthrow of the claims made on behalf of false gods. Such a theme, though not prominent in Nahum, is characteristic of the denunciation of Assyria in Isa. 10.

Two concluding comments concerning this acrostic poem may be in order. First, as we have seen from a number of the phrases used, it seems clear that the poem employs much of the vocabulary characteristic of the Jerusalem cult. The links we have noted have for the most part been with the Psalms or Isaiah, both thoroughly Jerusalemite collections, and with Amos, whose vocabulary may reflect Jerusalemite origins. We cannot tell whether this was a newly composed poem, reusing such language and imagery, or whether the links are more direct and an existing liturgical piece has been taken over; in either event, we are able to detect something of the origins of what is here expressed so vividly. Second, by placing the poem in its present context following v. 1, "concerning Nineveh," a specific application has been given to what originally may have been of more general reference. That is not to say that such application was in any way illegitimate; of what point could it be to announce that Yahweh would punish his enemies if no indication of those enemies was ever given? Whereas in such Psalms as Pss. 2 and 110 a generalized promise of the overthrow of enemies is made, here that promise has been given a specific application. The point is of some significance in our interpretation, insofar as many Bible readers are untroubled by the kind of denunciation of evil which can be spiritualized but find themselves uneasy when the enemies are specifically identified. In the OT, prophets such as Amos do not hesitate to name specific peoples who are the objects of God's wrath (Amos 1 – 2); in the NT Jesus does the same thing (Matt. 23). The OT also contains a more extended example of the same process in 2 Kgs. 18 – 19, where the traditional motifs are applied to the rebuttal of Sennacherib's threat against Jerusalem.

9-11 These verses allow us to see that the application of words of judgment against Nineveh was not the only possible understanding to which they could be put. Here the community itself appears to be under judgment. It should however be noted that the precise interpretation of these verses remains obscure; one need only look at the drastic rearrangement undertaken by the NEB to see how far from agreement the scholarly world has been concerning their meaning. The judgment of Simon John DeVries that "this is surely one of the most obtuse passages in the Old Testament" would be widely supported ("The Acrostic of Nahum," 479). He is surely right in rejecting any attempt at tracing the continuation of the acrostic here and in seeing these verses as prose rather than poetry; more questionable is his rejection of the interrogative form in favor of an "indefinite" use of the word *ma* to mean "whatever" rather than "what."

9 The section begins with an accusing word directed against those who "plot against the LORD," an expression characteristically found with reference to those within the community who should have known better rather than a foreign enemy (Pss. 35:4; 41:7; RSV "imagine the worst for me"). "He will make a full end" is a phrase very similar to that found (and translated identically in the RSV) in v. 8; this similarity may account for the placing of this obscure fragment at this point on a kind of "catchword" principle.

But the RSV translation of the last part of the verse, involving as it does a translation based on the LXX at one point and a gratuitous emendation at another, is unlikely. It seems more likely that the rather literal rendering of the RV is nearer the mark: "affliction shall not rise up the second time." The point being made is the certainty and completeness of Yahweh's looked-for vengeance or judgment on those who oppose his will. If, as is likely, the words of Nahum reached substantially their final form during the Exile, it would be easy to see how this destruction could be understood as having taken place — as thoroughly as the overthrow of Nineveh itself.

10 A series of similes is then added to illustrate this completeness of destruction. The phrase translated "entangled thorns" is not certain in meaning, for the adjective occurs nowhere else in this form. These words and the next pair (whose meaning is even more obscure) seem to have been chosen more on grounds of assonance than to convey a precisely definable message; the Hebrew words *sirim sebukim* and *sabeam sebu'im* share similar consonantal sounds. The apparent meaning of the text would imply a reference to drunkards, as is noted in the RSV margin ("drunken as with their drink"), but most translations and commentaries have either emended the text or omitted the phrase entirely. An attractive emendation is that of DeVries ("The Acrostic of Nahum," 480), reading *sobebim* for *sabeam* ("brambles"). In any case, whether the imagery is of God's anger as a raging fire among dry thorns and brambles, or whether it is of his enemies being overcome when besotted with drink, the message is that of certain devastation to those who oppose him.

11 Though differently structured from what has preceded, this verse also seems to be aimed against Yahweh's enemies who plot evil against him even when they should know better. In the RSV translation this is again expressed in the form of a question, a form which is reached by a minor emendation of the Hebrew text. There the last word of v. 10, *male* ("filled"), makes no apparent sense in the context, so it has been emended to *halo* ("did one not") and transferred to the beginning of v. 11. There can be no certainty as to the rightness of such changes, but something of the kind is needed to make sense of the passage, which then becomes reasonably straightforward. Here, as often in the prophets, we have an accusation aimed against any who would attempt to thwart Yahweh's purpose by plotting evil. The particular word used to describe such plotting (*hosheb*, "plotted"; *yo'ets*, "counseled") have sometimes been taken as characteristic of a definable class of wise men in Israel, but Norman Whybray has shown the dangers implicit in such categorization (*The Intellectual Tradition in the OT*). Basically the theme here, as in a number of other passages, is the more general one of Yahweh's supremacy over the plots and devices of all human counselors and worldly expertise, whose certain fate has been vividly described in v. 10.

12-15 With these verses we pass to difficulties of a different kind. In vv. 9-11 the main problem related to the reliability of the text and its frame of reference. In vv. 12-15 text and translation are relatively straightforward, but difficulties arise from the apparently violent oscillation between promise and condemnation found within these verses. Not surprisingly, the RSV prints v. 14 with a space both before and after it, for its harsh threat contrasts very markedly with the promise found in vv. 12-13 and v. 15. The NEB alters the order of the verses to 13, 14, 12, 15, partly because of its attempt to trace the acrostic as far as v. 14. Many emendations have been proposed by commentators ever since J. M. Powis Smith in 1911, who suggested that v. 14 stood apart from the immediate context and was the first of Nahum's own oracles. Relevant also is John H. Eaton's comment that "the rapid changes in the person addressed certainly suggest some use of gesture and symbols to clarify the meaning" (*Vision in Worship*, 17). Prophecy was a living part of Israel's existence, and not simply a matter of written or even spoken words; nevertheless, we should also bear in mind that such grammatical obscurities are a rare phenomenon in the prophetic corpus.

With these general considerations in mind, we may begin a more detailed study of these verses by noting that the apparent oracular form of the section is not maintained throughout. Verse 12 contains the usual messenger formula "Thus says the LORD," and v. 13 maintains, somewhat awkwardly, the form of a prophetic oracle. In v. 14, however, Yahweh is referred to in the 3rd person, and the object of the address is also different. It seems probable, therefore, that the contents of these verses are of diverse origin, and that they have been drawn together thematically. Thus, words of promise in vv. 12-13 are balanced by the threat in v. 14, and v. 15 serves to emphasize that the maintenance of right cultic observance was, to say the least, one important ingredient in the preservation of Israel's right relation with Yahweh. For such a passage purely form-critical analysis must inevitably be inadequate. It is noteworthy also that this section well illustrates the difficulty in deciding whether or not Nahum is appropriately described as a cult prophet. Here as elsewhere cultic themes are used and the importance of the festal liturgical round stressed; but neither here nor elsewhere is there any suggestion that proper observance of the cult provides an automatic guarantee of divine favor and salvation.

12 The messenger formula is clear enough; the difficulty here relates to the meaning of the phrase that follows. The point may be illustrated by reference to the diversity of modern translations: e.g., RSV "Though they be strong and many"; NEB "Has the punishment been so great?" The difficulty is not a new one; already at the time of the LXX translation there must have been some uncertainty, for by omitting one word and redividing the consonants of the remainder, a reference is found to the one who rules over many waters. Clearly in such a situation a generally accepted solution is unattainable, but it seems most probable that the RSV is broadly right, and that the reference is to the enemies of Yahweh, whose punishment is assured despite their apparent strength. This would make sense of the following line, "they will be cut off and pass away," though some emendation is again needed, since the verb "pass away" is singular.

In the last part of the verse the RSV translation envisages a contrast between the "they" who are to be punished and the "you" (feminine, for Judah) who are not to be afflicted again. Alternatively it has been suggested that the verb 'anah might have the meaning "smite," with the feminine "you" referring to Nineveh and the sense that one blow will be decisive, but this seems less likely than the contrast implied in the RSV rendering. If this is so, we have here a characteristic promise of respite from future punishment of the kind that the people had so often experienced in the past. Here once again the relevance of such a word of assurance in the situation of exile is obvious, and the most natural thematic comparison is with Isa. 40–55. The actual word *'anah* ("afflict") is, however, particularly characteristic of the Psalms of lament; cf. Ps. 88:7; 102:23, where the verb is translated "overwhelm" and "broken" respectively.

13 "And now" is a characteristic introduction to an especially solemn part of the prophetic word. The verse as a whole underlines the theme of deliverance already set out at the end of v. 12. The image of rescue from the yoke of the oppressor provides another link between Nahum and the Isaiah tradition; the same metaphor is used in Isa. 9:4; 10:27; and 14:25, in each case with reference to Assyrian domination. The "yoke" was the wooden frame which linked together a pair of animals; its metaphorical meaning is the inescapability of being under the yoke. The figure is extended with a reference to the breaking of bonds. Even if the usage is figurative, we are reminded of the horrors of military domination, which were no more attractive in the ancient world than today.

14 The "you" here being addressed is masculine, but we should not need this grammatical clue to recognize that there is a clear difference from v. 13; punishment rather than consolation is now the theme. It is possible, as we have already seen, that the verses in this section have come to be disordered, but it may also be that the alternation of consolation for Israel and threats against their enemies is a deliberate one. In any case no attempt will here be made to suggest any different order; such a suggestion would in any case have to remain at an entirely hypothetical level.

The introductory phrase "The LORD has given commandment about you" serves to emphasize the solemnity of what is to follow, while bearing out that God both judges and redeems through his word of command. The text offers no specific indication of the identity of "you." The natural understanding in the larger context of the book as a whole would be that the words must refer to Assyria or to Nineveh. But it is possible, as has been suggested by Jörg Jeremias, that material of this type was originally aimed against the people of Israel and only subsequently reinterpreted so as to apply to Nineveh (*Kulturprophetie und Gerichtsverkündigung*, 20-25). It is certainly true that some of the threats here correspond closely to condemnations of Israelite religious malpractice found elsewhere in the OT.

Before looking at such parallels, we should note that the meaning of the first line of the accusation is not entirely clear. A literal rendering would be "It will not be sown from your name any more." Kevin J. Cathcart has proposed reading the *min-* ("from") as part of the verb, thus making "your name" the subject: "your name will not . . ." (*Nahum in the Light of Northwest Semitic*, 67). But this suggestion is weakened by the parallel with "from the house" in the next line. It seems best to take the text as it stands, with "sown" referring to the continuation of the group addressed, as in RSV "perpetuated." In other words, we have here a warning of complete extinction.

It is the next section which provides links with other OT condemnations of Israel. The phrase *mibbeth eloheyka* is naturally to be translated "from the house of your gods" (as in the RSV), if the context is understood as a condemnation of the Assyrians. But if the original thrust was against Israel, then *elohim* here, as often, might be plural in form but singular in meaning. The reference would then be to the temple, and we should then have an attack upon Israel's own practice of a kind familiar from many prophetic passages (cf. Isa. 1:11ff.). The condemnation of the "graven image and the molten image" could also be seen as having originally been aimed against Israel itself. The former is condemned in the Decalogue (Exod. 20:4) and in such prophetic judgments as Hos. 11:2 (RSV "idols") and Mic. 1:7 (RSV "images"); the latter is found both in narratives (Exod. 32, the golden calf; Judg. 17 – 18, the discreditable origins of the sanctuary at Dan) and in prophetic oracles (Hos. 13:2). There is, therefore, some prima facie evidence for accepting Jeremias's proposals that these condemnations were originally "words of judgment against Israel." On the other hand, there are too many imponderables for us to be really confident concerning so drastic a reshaping of the material. Not least, we should need to ask why such a development has taken place with Nahum and not with other prophets whose words have been preserved. For this and other reasons set out in more detail by Hermann Schulz (*Das Buch Nahum*, 141-44), we should perhaps accept it as more likely that these words have always been addressed to Israel's enemies and then applied specifically to Assyria when the book reached its final form.

Consideration has not yet been given to the last section of this verse. Again modern translations differ sharply: RSV "I will make your grave, for you are vile"; NEB "I will grant you burial, fickle though you have been." (It should also be remembered that in NEB this verse is immediately followed by v. 12, and that the clauses which comprise this verse have been reordered.) The basic problem relates to the word *qallota* ("vile" or "fickle"). Anyone so described is regarded as of no consequence, worthless; and so a note of condemnation seems to be implied. To that extent the RSV is nearer the mark. Perhaps the best sense is achieved by another minor amendment, reading *ashim* (from the root *sh-m-m*) for the first verb *asim*, thus "I will devastate your grave, for you are worthless" (Cathcart, *Nahum in the Light of Northwest Semitic*, 67). This would make a natural conclusion to the threats of the rest of the verse; desecration of the burial place was always regarded with particular horror in the ancient Near East (cf. the account of the burial of Saul, 1 Sam. 31).

15 This verse (which begins ch. 2 in the Hebrew text) reverts once again to the saving purpose of God touched on in v. 13. After the opening *hinneh* ("behold") the first part of the verse is identical with Isa. 52:7a. Speculation whether one prophetic collection may have borrowed from the other is not very profitable, and such a purely mechanical relation in any case seems inherently unlikely. Rather, as was suggested in the Introduction, it is more probable that there was a stock of oracular material which might be used as appropriate in the particular circumstances of each collection. In Isa. 52, it is clear that the circumstance was the coming deliverance of the exiled Israelites from Babylonian oppression; here the deliverance was from the Assyrian yoke. To express such a conviction, the language used was that of Yahweh's solemn entry into his sanctuary, an ancient hymnic motif which was clearly of direct relevance to a time of historical threat.

We might regard it as inherently probable that such a theme of Yahweh's epiphany would most naturally find expression in cultic worship. But if there were any doubts, these should be removed by the next line, "Keep your feasts, O Judah." Though the noun "feasts" is plural, it seems likely that the primary reference is to the autumn festival, the feast par excellence. Much scholarly attention has been devoted to attempts to reconstruct the basic elements of this festival, with conspicuously little agreement, but it does seem probable that one such element will have been the proclamation of the kingship of Yahweh. Such a proclamation is of fundamental theological significance for the understanding of Nahum, for a basic theme of the book is the assertion of Yahweh's sovereignty over all the forces of the nations opposed to him. The particular thrust may be aimed at Assyria, but it seems likely that much of the material could have been of a traditional nature with no specific anti-Assyrian reference. Equally, as subsequent use of this and other prophetic collections has demonstrated, reapplication of the proclamation that Yahweh is King over against quite different hostile powers was legitimate.

Israel had its own part to play in this: "fulfil your vows." The reference is primarily, though not exclusively, to the solemn obligations laid upon the people of God to maintain his proper worship. The final promise recalls once more Isa. 52. Here the promise is more general ("for never again shall the wicked come against you"), whereas in Isa. 52:1b it is more specific ("for there shall no more come into you the uncircumcised and the unclean"). In fact the two phrases are more closely akin than the RSV translation might suggest, differentiated only by the use of different verbs ("come," "come against") and the greater specificity of Isaiah. Here as elsewhere in Isa. 40– 55 there is a strongly nationalistic strain; what in Nahum is expressed in general terms against the wicked is narrowed down in Deutero-Isaiah to a specific condemnation of those who failed to meet the specific cultic conditions laid upon Israel. The comparison is ironic, in view of the usual reputation of Nahum as narrowly nationalistic and Deutero-Isaiah as holding a universal vision.

The final phrase of this key verse, "he is utterly cut off," may be understood in two ways. It might be a so-called "prophetic perfect," expressing future hope in terms of present reality. As such it would form part of the promise of exclusion of the wicked already formulated in the previous line. More probably, however, since it appears to stand outside the metrical structure of this section, it is an elaboration intended to take this general statement and apply it specifically to Nineveh by declaring that Nineveh is about to fall.

CHAPTER 2

1 In this verse it is clear that the "you" being addressed has once again changed. Here once more we have the switch from Judah, the recipient of God's blessing, to the object of his condemnation, an object soon to be specifically identified as Nineveh.

Precisely how this condemnation is envisaged is not very clear, setting aside the more general recognition that throughout Nahum we have to do with poetic and figurative language rather than precise objective analysis. Destruction is to come about through "the shatterer." This seems to be a rather free rendering by the RSV. The usual meaning of the Hebrew verb *puts* is "to scatter" or "disperse," which might imply military conquest, hence the RV translation, "he that dasheth to pieces." But consideration should be given to an emendation of the vowels of the Hebrew word from *mephits* to *mappets*, a "club" or "hammer." This may underlie both the RSV and the NEB rendering "the battering-ram."

It is noteworthy that the only certain occurrence of the word *mappets* in the Hebrew Bible is at Jer. 51:20, and this section of Nahum has much in common with Jer. 51. There the certainty of destruction is announced for Babylon; here Nineveh is the object. It is very likely that the same imagery would be invoked in changing circumstances, and it is possible that such imagery originated in a cultic context. Before engaging in battle, Israel would invoke divine power against its enemies.

The remainder of the verse clearly uses military terminology; less clear is the impression it is intended to convey. Probably the instructions are to be understood ironically. Yahweh himself is "the scatterer" (or the ultimate wielder of the club, if we emend the text) of the first part of the verse, and in the face of such an enemy all military preparations are useless. The foreign nations oracles at the end of Jeremiah would again supply the nearest

35

parallel; Jer. 46:3-4 urges the completion of military preparations, knowing that they will be rendered useless by the disaster
alluded to in vv. 5-6. The same ironic mode of expression is found
again in Nahum, at 3:14, though the grammatical form in the
two cases differs somewhat. Here a series of Hebrew infinitives
functions as imperatives, commanding the defenders of the city
to make all possible preparations against attack.

2   If this understanding of v. 1b as intended ironically is correct,
then the bracketing of v. 2 (as in the RSV) or its being placed
between 1:15 and 2:1 (as in the NEB) becomes unnecessary. It
can instead be seen as making clear the reason for the uselessness
of the preparations. Yahweh himself is about to inflict upon his
enemies the same kind of treatment as the "plunderers" have
brought upon Israel. The verb translated "is restoring" may have
a military reference (cf. Ps. 126:1), but it frequently has wider
implications also.

Many commentators have emended *geon* ("majesty") to *gephen*
("vine") (cf. BHS), thus providing a suitable antecedent to
"branches" at the end of the verse. It is undoubtedly the case
that Israel is often referred to as a vine (e.g., Ps. 80), and it might
be argued that the repetition of *geon*, referring to both "Jacob"
and "Israel," has led to a textual error. But such emendation is
not necessary; repetition is a regular feature of Hebrew poetry
and seems likely to be deliberate here. Less certain is whether
"Jacob" and "Israel" are intended to refer to the two kingdoms.
This is clearly implied by the NEB translation, "The LORD will
restore the pride of Jacob and Israel alike." This interpretation
has been advocated by some commentators (see the discussion
in W. Rudolph, *Micha, etc.*, 160), but it seems unlikely, for nowhere else are the two kingdoms clearly delineated in this way.
More probably, as in Isa. 40 – 55, "Jacob" and "Israel" are synonyms, with the repetition having the effect of expressing a totality.

The phraseology of the last part of the verse is also striking,
and again we find a link with the Isaiah tradition. The same
Hebrew root (*b-q-q*) underlies the words translated "plunderers"
and "stripped"; this same rare verb is found in Isa. 24:1, 3 (RSV
"lay waste"), where it depicts Yahweh's action as he himself lays
waste the earth. We are reminded of the difficulty of dating material of this kind. Isaiah 24 is part of the so-called Isaiah Apoc-

alypse, and is usually regarded as the latest part of that book. But much of the language used, as here in Nahum, has ancient roots, ultimately of mythic origin and embodied in Israel's proclamation in worship of the mighty acts of God.

3-12 After the uncertainties of the preceding verses it is a relief to turn in vv. 3-12 to a poem which, while certainly not without its difficulties, seems clearly to be an organized unity. It represents one of the finest examples in the OT of this particular literary form, the poem celebrating the defeat of the enemy army. The overall structure of poems of this kind is clear enough; at first the prowess of the army is described, so as to make all the more vivid the following descriptions of the chaos brought about by its overthrow. Such poems may well have had their origin in the cult, where they would have been used as a hoped-for means of bringing about the desired result. For the most part, however, in their OT usage they are either applied to a specific foreign enemy, as is the case here, with its direct reference to Nineveh, or transformed into the universal language of apocalyptic.

3 This initial verse is clearly an account of the awe-inspiring power of the enemy army. It is not easy to decide how much of the imagery is traditional and how much derives from actual experience of Assyrian practice. Though most commentaries have tended toward the latter view, it may well be that many of the terms here used are conventional and could be applied to any army. Certainty in the matter is impossible. In this verse we find reference to the characteristic features of the hostile force: "shield," military uniform, "chariots," "chargers." The predominance of red in the imagery of the verse may be due to the empirical fact that red uniforms and accoutrements were customary, or the allusion may be to the imagined presence of blood as the result of previous victories gained by the terrifying army. It is noteworthy that Ezek. 23:6 uses similar language, and the same doubt concerning the appropriate type of understanding is present there also.

One word in particular has presented difficulty to interpreters. Hebrew *peladot* is translated "like flame" in the RSV, with a note in the margin that this implies the correction of a Hebrew word of uncertain meaning; the NEB has "flickering" and older versions "steel." The Jewish medieval commentators admitted their uncertainty about this word; of the many suggestions that have been made perhaps as likely as any is that which would see a link with a similar Ugaritic word referring to decorations of the chariots (R. Vuilleumier and C. A. Keller, *Michée, etc.*, 121). Even this remains quite uncertain, for the reading of the Ugaritic text is disputed.

The phrase translated "in array" has also been questioned, and is regarded as a possible gloss in the Hebrew text. But it would be wrong to delete it, for it forms part of the picture of the overall build-up of military might. Again there is a link with Jer. 51, this time with v. 12, where the RSV reads "prepare the ambushes." More difficult is the last phrase of Nah. 2:3, rendered by the RSV "the chargers prance" — a far cry from the KJV translation, "and the fir trees shall be terribly shaken." That *berosh* normally means a tree of some kind is beyond question; the only dispute is whether it is a fir, a cypress, or a juniper. Such a meaning gives no acceptable sense here, and the question becomes one of deciding whether to emend the text or to suppose some figurative use of the word. The latter view is supported by Kevin J. Cathcart, who translates "spears," and suggests that they were probably made of wood (*Nahum in the Light of Northwest Semitic*, 89). A wooden spear would presumably not be particularly effective; therefore the reference would be to its shaft, as already proposed tentatively in the Koehler-Baumgartner lexicon. But perhaps this is a case where an emendation is more likely. By substitution of a "p" for the "b" in the Hebrew word, the reading *happarashim* is obtained. This change is suggested by BHS and has been accepted by the RSV. The word would then mean "chargers." The LXX reading *hoi hippeis* ("the horsemen") gives additional support to this proposal.

4 The account of the awe-inspiring character of the hostile army continues. To the innocent bystander the chariotry could often appear as the deadliest danger of all. Each of the three verbs in this verse are of the somewhat unusual form which involves a doubling of one of the root letters, and this usage is surely deliberately embarked upon for its onomatopoeic effect: *yitholelu, yishtaqshequn, yerotsetsu* (Muilenburg, "A Study in Hebrew Rhetoric:

Repetition and Style," *Supplements to Vetus Testamentum* 1 (1953): 97-111).

5 This genre, where we have a description of the overthrow of the enemy army, does not employ a sudden dramatic switch away from its awesome character to its destruction. Rather, we become aware in the course of the account that something is going wrong; the disciplined movement becomes disorderly, the regular advance falters and then becomes a headlong rout. Jeremiah 46:3-5 provides a vivid example of such writing. "The officers are summoned" (RSV's understanding of a somewhat obscure original may be accepted, emending the active verb of the Hebrew into a passive; cf. BHS) is neutral in expression; it may be that some new advance might result from the summons. But the next phrase gives a clear indication that all is not well with the supposedly invincible army: "they stumble as they go." Hebrew *kashal* regularly has the sense of unsteady progress, and what is implied here is either a sense of desperation or uncertainty as to what the next move should be.

The first instinct of those halted in their previously unstoppable advance is to look to their defenses: "the wall" and the *sokek*. The Hebrew word *homah* can mean a wall in the literal sense of the defenses of a city, or it can be used figuratively of any means of protection; if the interpretation assumed here is correct, the latter sense will be the more natural in this context. As for *sokek*, the RSV's choice of "mantelet" seems odd, for it is not a word in everyday English use. The idea again is of some kind of defensive position, and the usage is probably again metaphorical, as it is in Ps. 140:7 where the verbal form from the same root is found (RSV "thou hast covered [my head]").

The interpretation here offered implies that these verses tell of the overthrow of the hitherto invincible Assyrian army, using a recognized literary form found elsewhere in the OT (e.g., Jer. 46, as above, and Isa. 10:27c-34). It should be noted that other commentators have supposed that at least up to the first part of this verse the reference has been to the army of Yahweh. Thus John H. Eaton summarizes this verse as portraying how "the divine commander re-forms his troops for the assault on the last bastion" (*Vision in Worship*, 18; cf. also Vuilleumier and Keller, *Michée, etc.*,

119-23, who envisage a series of distinct poems juxtaposed together). Similarly, in this verse BHS suggests the insertion of a
negative before the reference to this stumbling, presumably on
the grounds that the forces of Yahweh himself could not be thought
of as stumbling.

Such an understanding undeniably makes the best sense if the
total picture is to be viewed quasi-historically, with the sum-
moning to mind first of the army, then of the city it is besieging.
If the city is Nineveh, the army must of necessity be of Assyria's
enemy: Yahweh himself. But it may be questioned whether so
logical a reconstruction is justified. Assyria is regularly pictured
in the OT as a military power (cf. Isa. 10:5ff.). To envisage its
overthrow inevitably meant the defeat of its hitherto invincible
army. This, coupled with the fact that the form of the overthrow
of the enemy army is, as we have seen, a recognizable one in the
OT, leads us to suppose that the interpretation set out above may
be preferable, though it would be foolish in any case to suppose
that certainty is possible. We shall discover a similar ambiguity
when we come to the depiction of the lions later in this chapter.

6 However the preceding verses be understood, it is generally
agreed that vv. 6-9 picture the fall of the hated enemy city, iden-
tifed in v. 8 as Nineveh. Those who take the army of vv. 3-5 as
that of Yahweh himself suppose that the scene has now changed
to the panic-stricken defenders. But it is at least as plausible to
see continuity: first the confident army, then the uncertainties
leading to a concern for defense, now the recognition that it is too
late even for defensive measures — there is no security anywhere.

"The river gates are opened" is a phrase which has often been
discussed in terms of the precise way in which Nineveh is supposed to have been overthrown, as if a poem of this kind could
provide precise historical or geographical information. The temp-
tation to seek such information from the book of Nahum has been
increased by the fact that the Babylonian Chronicle, our primary
source for reconstructing the historical outline of the period, is
damaged at this point. In fact, the archaeological evidence makes
it likely that the destruction of Nineveh was by burning rather
than by flood or by tampering with the water supply. In any
case, though the date of Nahum is very uncertain, it seems more

likely that he prophesied before rather than after the fall of Nineveh in 612.

We should recognize, therefore, that we are dealing here with poetry and not with a historical account. It may be that such an expression as "the river gates are opened" is intended to imply betrayal, the gates being open for the enemy to enter. Or it may imply flooding, if we think of sluice gates controlling the water supply. But again we should be cautious of supposing any detailed topographical knowledge on the prophet's part. This becomes even more apparent in the remainder of this verse, "the palace is in dismay," which translated more literally would be "the palace melts." The figurative language might be understood of the actual destruction of the palace (NEB "the palace topples down"). Or, as is often the case with the verb *mug*, especially in the Psalms, it may imply the complete breakup of the established order (cf. Ps. 75:3 RSV "the earth totters").

7 From now on it is clear that military might is irrelevant to save the city; disaster has struck, and attention focuses upon the effects of that disaster. So much is clear. Unfortunately, this verse is one of the many in Nahum where the exact force of some of the words and phrases remains in dispute.

The KJV translation of this verse begins, "And Huzzab shall be led away captive," implying that the Hebrew word *hutstsab* was a proper name. Modern commentators are agreed that this is not so, but their agreement ends there. The RSV rendering "its mistress is stripped" is accompanied by a marginal note that the meaning of the Hebrew is uncertain; NEB "the train of captives goes into exile" is dependent upon an article by Godfrey Rolles Driver which was effective in its dismissal of the traditional rendering but less convincing in its proposed alternative ("Farewell to Queen Huzzab!" *Journal of Theological Studies* n.s. 15 [1964]: 296-98). Many other suggestions have been made concerning the meaning of the word or for more drastic emendation of the text.

Whatever the original of the word, it is clear that she (the subject must be feminine to agree with the following verbs) undergoes the humiliation of being "stripped," perhaps of royal robes, and "carried off." There follows the use of a device found elsewere in the OT, underlining a point being made about the women of the royal court by providing a role for the queen's attendants (cf. Judg. 5:29). Again there is some doubt as to the way in which their fate is described. If the Hebrew word *mena-hagot* comes from the usual root *nahag*, meaning "to drive," usually of animals, it should probably be emended to a passive form; the picture would be of the delicate women of the court being herded off like animals. It is, however, possible that a second root *nahag* ("to moan") is here used, and this would justify the RSV translation, "her maidens lamenting."

There follow two characteristic figures expressive of mourning: the sound of a dove is often described as comparable with the ritual "moaning" of mourners at a funeral; and the gesture of "beating their breasts" is an even more widespread gesture of lamentation. This remains true even though the particular phrase actually used here is not the customary one. "Drumming upon their hearts" would be a more literal translation.

8 What has long been implicit is now explicitly stated: the subject of this vivid poem is "Nineveh." As in the book of Jonah, Nineveh as the capital city stands for the whole heathen empire which is under God's judgment. But whereas in Jonah that empire repents and is spared, here nothing intervenes to prevent the judgment being fully worked out. The actual description of the city which follows is vivid though somewhat obscure. The Hebrew text of the verse contains the letter "m" nine times in eight words; it is not easy to decide whether this is a deliberate literary device or is the result of some corruption in the transmission of the text. (The alternatives are perhaps not mutually exclusive). Basically, it seems probable that we have an allusion back to v. 6, with its water imagery; in each case the use of water as a familiar picture of the threat of the return of chaos may be traced.

The phrase "whose waters run away" contains two difficulties. First, it should be noted that the RSV translation here implies an emendation which follows the LXX in referring to "waters" rather than to "days" as in the MT (the words are very similar in Hebrew). Second, it is not clear whether the waters have risen up to overwhelm the city or have "run away." Logically the former might seem the more natural meaning, but probably the kaleidoscopic imagery found in the prophet has now switched from the waters as instruments of destruction to waters as the source of Nineveh's wealth — all now dissipated. There may also be an allusion to the kind of thought represented by Ps. 114:3, where, confronted with the mighty acts of Yahweh, "the sea looked and fled" — the same verb as is here translated "run away." No power is adequate to stand before the majesty of Yahweh.

The remainder of the verse can best be seen as offering further support to the interpretation of vv. 3-5 offered above. It reverts to the theme of the army whose first appearance had seemed so devastating, but which is now in disarray. The attempt to stop the rout (" 'Halt! Halt!' they cry") is useless; "none turns back." The utter panic which seizes the enemies against whom Yahweh is waging war is a regular theme of "holy war" episodes in the OT (cf. Judg. 7:21; 2 Kgs. 7:6-7).

Both in this verse and in the next the repeated imperatives ("Halt! Halt!" "Plunder . . . plunder") are reminiscent of Isa. 40–66, where this particular literary usage is very common (e.g., Isa. 40:1).

9 The theme of this verse is the plunderer plundered. Again, a characteristic feature of holy war stories is a description of the defeated army in its demoralized condition, leaving behind the treasure that it had acquired (cf. 2 Kgs. 7). Here in chaotic flight the once invincible army has abandoned its ill-gotten "silver" and "gold." "There is no end of treasure" is a phrase almost identical in the RSV with Isa. 2:7 (though before claiming yet another link with the Isaiah tradition we should note that the words for "treasure" differ, though the overall context is similar in both cases).

10-12 The poem concludes with three verses which stand somewhat apart from what has preceded. As we have already noted, it would be misleading to suppose that any part of this poem can be taken as a matter-of-fact description of empirical events. In these last verses, even more clearly than in what has preceded, the language is visionary. The utter rout of Yahweh's enemies is depicted, with a vivid series of images describing the ravages of lions. The first three words are alliterative in a fashion beloved of Hebrew but almost impossible to reproduce in acceptable English: *buqah umebuqah umebullaqah*. The "Desolate! Desolation and ruin!" of the RSV is a poor substitute. The poetic originality of Nahum is suggested by the fact that none of these forms appears elsewhere in the Hebrew Bible, though analogous forms are found in Isa. 24:1-3, with similar alliterative effect.

The vivid description continues by fastening on those parts of the body which were thought to react especially to disaster: heart, knees, loins, face. The picture is of the whole being thrown into disarray as the extent of the desolation is revealed.

11 In the context of this little poem it seems as if the effect has been described before the cause, for only now is the picture developed of the ravages of a lion as the metaphor for Yahweh's avenging work. Again the picture is built up with remarkable artistry, for at first we have only a series of questions, with no spelling out of the damage caused. The first question is clear enough, for the lion's *me'on* (literally, "stronghold") is clearly his den. The second is less clear, for it seems to speak of a place of pasture (cf. RSV mg.). Sense could be achieved by such a translation as "the feeding place of the young lions," but it is perhaps better to assume a corruption of the Hebrew text by metathesis (the transposition of two consonants in the Hebrew word) and to read *ma'arah* ("cave") instead of *mir'eh* ("place of pasture"). This is the solution followed by both the RSV and the NEB. In the remainder of the verse it is possible that we have an allusion to the conviction that Jerusalem would never be destroyed. Just as the lion could bring food to its den where the cubs would be undisturbed, so would Yahweh, it was believed, protect his people from all disturbance.

12 But a lion does not only guard its own young! In this last verse of the poem we revert once again to the damage done when the lion attacks its enemies. It has now become clear that this poem has two levels of meaning in its reference to a lion. Yahweh himself can be alluded to in the prophetic tradition as a lion (cf. the picture of his roaring in Amos 1:2 and the direct comparison made in Amos 3:8), and that tradition appears to have been in our prophet's mind in this poem. But it is also the case that Assyrian kings referred to themselves in their inscriptions as "lions," and that thought is also present and becomes more prominent in this verse.

Support for this link is found in another notable connection with the Isaiah tradition. Isaiah 5:29 pictures the onslaught of the Assyrian army in terms of an attack by lions, and some of the vocabulary (two of the words for "lion," *labi* and *kaphir*; *tereph*, "prey") is common to the two passages, as well as the form of the closing assertion, "with none to . . . " (cf. Nah. 2:11). In this section, the primary concern is with Assyria as the lion; but whereas in Isaiah, a century earlier than Nahum, the image had been employed as a threat to the prophet's own people, here the point is that the once-dreaded lion is itself now to be a prey. Once again we see how Nahum used what was probably a part of a common stock of metaphorical language, perhaps rooted in the cultic usage of Jerusalem.

The destruction wrought by the lion is described in the most vivid terms. The use of the verb *hanaq* ("strangled"), elsewhere used only of Ahithophel's suicide at 2 Sam. 17:23, may not seem especially appropriate to describe a lion's dispatch of its victim; nevertheless, it conveys something of the exultation of the poet in the fact that even those who seem most powerful are themselves the victims of God's power. The vigor of the poetic imagination here is also shown by the use of no fewer than four different words for lions; the English translation inevitably cannot match such rich variety.

13 This brief additional oracle is linked to what has preceded by the catchword "young lions" (*kephirim*), found also in v. 11; but it is certainly not a simple continuation of what has preceded. Translations and commentators differ as to whether it is prose or poetry, and as to whether it is better understood as an epilogue to the preceding poem or as an introduction to what follows. Thus, while Cathcart, for example, takes it as "the culmination of the unit" (*Nahum in the Light of Northwest Semitic*, 109), Eaton understands it as the opening of a new series of utterances stretching through ch. 3 (*Readings in Biblical Hebrew*, 2: 84). That some dislocation has taken place is clear from the way in which the Hebrew text contains both 2nd- and 3rd-person suffixes referring to the same object (cf. RSV mg., which shows that "her chariots" in the original has been modified to obtain a smoother English rendering).

It may be wisest to regard this verse as an independent fragment, a prophetic oracle introduced by a phrase originally characteristic of single combat and found with special frequency in

Ezekiel: "I am coming at you" is one suggested translation (M. Greenberg, *Ezekiel 1-20*, 113). But whereas in Ezekiel the formula is directed against Israel, here it is applied to Nineveh, and this is elaborated in a series of expressions characteristic of the language of holy war. In particular, the theme is one found several times in the Psalms, of chariots as a false basis for human trust. Psalm 46:9 uses similar ideas, and 20:7 expressly refers to the falsity of trust in the power of chariots. Then, with an abrupt change of metaphor, Nineveh is described as a young lion whose power is destroyed by the sword of Yahweh.

The last phrase, "the voice of your messengers shall no more be heard," may seem something of an anticlimax. It has often been emended, particularly because the suffix which expresses the personal pronoun ("*your* messengers") has an anomalous form. But the basic sense of the text may be accepted as it stands. Messengers from the Assyrian king were not simply bringers of information; rather, they symbolized the threat that failure to conform to the demand implicit in their message would bring swift and disastrous punishment from the great king of Assyria. Much of the point of 2 Kgs. 18 – 19 turns on the way in which the messengers' certainty that they could impose terms on defenseless Judah was subjected to a dramatic overthrow.

CHAPTER 3

1-19 Most of the references to Nineveh thus far have been allusive rather than direct. Much of the language has been based on what is found in Isaiah and the Psalms, both strongly Jerusalemite collections. Thus it is likely that terms which might be used of any enemy who dared to resist the power of Yahweh have been taken up with a clear, but for the most part indirect, reference to Nineveh. From this point on, the allusions become more specific; there remains no room for doubt as to the identity of the "bloody city."

The form used in this chapter is the "woe," which characteristically begins with the Hebrew word *hoi* ("woe"). There has been much dispute as to the setting in life from which this frequent prophetic form originated (J. Vermeylen, *Du prophète Isaïe à l'apocalyptique*, 2: 603-52). Most probably it is to be understood as a cry of mourning, and that makes good sense here. Whether Nahum was anticipating the expected fall of Nineveh or was rejoicing in an event that had already taken place, it is easy to see how prophetic irony was at work here. The city that had symbolized the arrogant power of an empire which had supposed itself to be inviolable was now itself experiencing the fate it had imposed on others — ample opportunity for an ironic mourning song.

1 "Woe to the bloody city." The RSV has this phrase again at Ezek. 24:6, 9 (the underlying Hebrew is slightly different from that found here), and Ezek. 22:2 calls on the prophet to "judge the bloody city." In all these cases the "city" in question is Jerusalem. It has been argued, particularly by Jörg Jeremias, that this type of condemnation of Jerusalem was especially characteristic of the prophets of the late preexilic period, and that it was only at a later stage of the transmission of the words of Nahum

47

that their thrust was changed and directed against Nineveh (*Kult-prophetie und Gerichtsverkündigung*, 30-31). But just as in considering Nah. 2:13 we noted that Ezekiel had reapplied terminology originally aimed against Judah's enemies so as to show that Jerusalem was now Yahweh's enemy, so it is perhaps more likely that Ezekiel is the innovator in his application of this phrase. (Jeremias's view is discussed in detail and rejected by H. Schulz, *Das Buch Nahum,* esp. 146-50). Nor should we lose sight of the creative power of the OT prophets in applying God's word to the situation in which they found themselves. For Micah in the 8th cent. (see especially Mic. 3:10) and for Ezekiel in the 6th, it was right to condemn Jerusalem; for Nahum in the time of the Assyrian domination, Nineveh was the human power which claimed divine prerogatives and must be condemned.

In the phrase "all full of lies" the word translated "lies" has a wider signification than untruths. At Hos. 7:3 it is translated "treachery." It is in any case unlikely that Nahum has a particular episode in mind; his condemnations are wide-ranging, accusing Nineveh of all that is evil. With "plunder" at the end of the verse we have a link with the poem on the lions in Nah. 2:10-12 and its elaboration in v. 13, for the same root is found there four times (RSV "prey").

2 The military image in this and the next verse has caused this section to be regarded as a later elaboration by those who suppose that this poem was only secondarily applied to Nineveh. This argument is supported by the irregularities of the Hebrew meter at this point (Jeremias, *Kultprophetie und Gerichtsverkündigung,* 33). But our knowledge of Hebrew meter is still an insufficient basis for judgments of this kind, and it seems better to see this imagery as integral to the poem as a whole, a fitting development from the theme of the plundering lion. The staccato translation of the RSV brings out the effect of the Hebrew very well, for it is impressionistic rather than a precise description. For most of the phrases there is little doubt as to their meaning, the one important exception being the word translated "galloping"; the underlying Hebrew root is found only once elsewhere, in the Song of Deborah (Judg. 5:22), another vivid but obscure poem.

3 The irony of the prophet's words is again apparent here. At face value this looks like an account of the power of the Assyrian armies, illustrated by the grisly sight of "hosts of slain, heaps of corpses, dead bodies without end." But in the context of the poem as a whole it is clear that the "slain" and the "corpses" are those of the Assyrian army themselves. The genre is similar to that of 2:3-12, a description of the confidence of a heathen army which is about to be overthrown by an even mightier power. The form may originate from taunt songs aimed at weakening enemy morale (cf. David's mockery of Goliath at 1 Sam. 17:45-47, in reply to the Philistine's own taunts); modern propaganda knows plenty of comparable devices.

4 The imagery changes. Now the hated city is likened to a "harlot," a figure of speech whose most famous use in the Bible is in describing the fate of "Babylon" (Rome) in Rev. 18. But it is also used in the OT, and here again we have an example of the application to a foreign enemy of a form elsewhere used with reference to Israel itself. In Ezek. 16 and 23 Jerusalem is portrayed as a harlot in language even more direct and offensive than that found here. Again there are similarities with Isa. 40–55, notably in the taunt over Babylon in ch. 47. In the present context the allusion may be more specific, to the worship of the goddess Ishtar, which is often protrayed in strongly sexual terms. She is known in the OT as Ashkarou.

Of the general sense of the verse there is little doubt, but one word has caused difficulty. Hebrew *hammokeret* is translated in the RSV as "who betrays"; but this sense of the root *m-k-r* ("to sell") is very forced, and attempts to achieve a meaning by postulating a different root are not very satisfactory. Here it seems better to follow Wilhelm Rudolph (*Micha, etc.*, 175) and other commentators and to suppose that the "k" and the "m" have been transposed to give a form *hakkomeret* ("who ensnares").

5 The opening of this verse is identical with that of 2:13, and this is much more likely to be a deliberate rhetorical device than an accidental dittography. The repetition serves to emphasize the inevitability and divine verification of the impending judgment.

Nakedness was a matter of particular shame in the world of the OT. This is made clear from the first reference to the subject at Gen. 2:25, where the fact that "the man and his wife were both naked, and were not ashamed" is a noteworthy indication of the distance between humanity as originally created and its present unhappy condition. Particular care was taken to prevent any exposure which was regarded as unseemly in the cult, where God's presence was especially manifest (Exod. 20:26; cf. Michal's condemnation of David at 2 Sam. 6:20). And so the divine punishment is one that was elsewhere used against Israel (e.g., Jer. 13:22), but the closest parallel is, as so often in Nahum, with Isa. 40–55. The threat against Nineveh here is strikingly similar to that against Babylon at 47:3. In both cases it seems that a particularly bitter part of the punishment would be the assurance that the "nations" and "kingdoms," once contemptuously overrun by Assyria or Babylon, would now see their oppressor's miserable fate.

6   The torrent of abuse continues, in terms reminiscent of Nah. 1:14. Such robust condemnation is offensive to our ears, but we should remember that it is characteristic of the biblical (and not just the OT) world. In that world God's sovereignty is of such decisive importance that any threat to it is treated with the utmost contempt. Hebrew *shiqqutsim*, here translated "filth," may also convey the underlying idea of the fate reserved for those who put their trust in other gods. The last word in the verse is probably better understood as by the RSV ("gazingstock") than by the NEB ("excrement"), though this latter interpretation is found in Jewish medieval commentators.

7   The specific reference to "Nineveh," found in this section of the book for the first time, has led some commentators to see this verse as the beginning of a new poem and apply vv. 1-6 originally to Jerusalem, its application to Nineveh being a matter of later adaptation. But the wordplay in the Hebrew (*roi/roayik*, RSV "gazingstock"/"who look on you") suggests a closer link, and it seems better to understand this verse as finally making explicit what has become more and more apparent during the earlier part of the poem: the mighty power now dramatically condemned and cast aside is none other than Assyria, typified by Nineveh its capital. Whether this poem is written in eager anticipation of Nineveh's fall or that event had already taken place, the need for mourning is now spelled out with the same grim irony which pervades so much of this poem. The verb *nud*, literally "to shake the head" (RSV "bemoan"), is often used of the professional process of mourning which was regarded as appropriate after any untimely death; the "comforters" similarly would be those whose role it was to supply consolation in a time of bereavement. Once again Isa. 40–55 provides the most striking parallel, with the dramatic opening verses of ch. 40 announcing that Jerusalem, unlike Nineveh here, could properly be comforted.

8 There follows what appears to be the most specific historical reference in the whole book. "Thebes" (Heb. *No Amon*), nowadays known as Karnak or Luxor, some 530 km. (330 mi.) south of Cairo, was one of the greatest of Egyptian cities. Its religious role was of particular significance as the sanctuary of the god Amon. (There has been some dispute whether the reference here is specifically to Thebes, or whether *No Amon* might be a designation of the whole of Egypt, just as Nineveh stands for Assyria; on the whole, the nature of the following description makes the more precise identification the more probable). The high point of Assyrian advance against Egypt was attained in 663 B.C. when this sacred site was sacked by the armies of Ashurbanipal. This was, however, by no means the end of Thebes as a major center for Egyptian religious practice, and there is indeed some evidence to suggest that, in part at least, it was quickly restored. This fact poses something of a problem for the dating of Nahum, about which no specific comments have so far been offered. This verse, and those which follow, seem to picture the sack of Thebes as a relatively recent event, whose impact is still great. It has often been doubted whether this vividness would really be credible if the poem were written forty or fifty years later, when Thebes had largely been restored to its former splendor. An obvious possible answer is that the destruction of Thebes came to be regarded as symbolic, so that a reference to it naturally evoked a vision of the power of destruction. (In an analogous way politicians and others in Britain still from time to time evoke "Dunkirk," not as a flourishing Belgian port, but as symbolizing a crisis in the Second World War.) This may be so, but there is no other evidence of such symbolic significance being accorded to Thebes.

Another possibility, put forward by Duane L. Christensen

("The Acrostic of Nahum Reconsidered," *Zeitschrift für die alttes-tamentlichen Wissenschaft* 87 [1975]: 17-30), is that this poem was originally composed soon after the sack of Thebes — perhaps in connection with the revolt of Manasseh against Assyria which may be alluded to at 2 Chr. 33:10-11 — and was later incorporated into the main body of Nahum's oracles. A variation of this is the view of Carl A. Keller, who sees Nahum as exercising a political activity counseling resistance to Assyria when others assumed that such resistance had become hopeless (Vuilleumier and Keller, *Michée, etc.,* 105). But these suggestions are speculative; little can be traced with confidence of the detailed political circumstances of the mid-7th cent. or of their effect upon Judah.

In short, then, though it is clear that the sack of Thebes provides the starting point for this section, the allusion remains in many ways opaque. It is much less helpful than might be expected for the dating of the prophet himself, and we must be content to say that several possibilities remain open, with a date shortly before the fall of Nineveh the most likely. But the fact is that here, as elsewhere in Nahum, the characteristic feature is the literary use to which historical data are put. This means also that themes which cannot be accurate historically or geographically are juxtaposed for literary effect. Thus, the expression "her rampart a sea" cannot be taken literally, for Thebes is almost 645 km. (400 mi.) from the nearest sea, but it summons up the idea of Yam, the primordial sea whose power is overthrown by Yahweh. Just as in Isa. 51:9-11 the themes of creation and deliverance at the Red Sea are woven together, so here creation language is used in the picture of the destruction of any human power that sets itself up in opposition to God.

9 Similar ideas are found in this verse. Perhaps the closest parallel is in Ps. 68:31, where "Egypt" and "Ethiopia" are again used — not so much as geographical designations but as symbolizing former enemies now rendered harmless by the power of God. One strand of tradition, found in Isa. 11:11 and 19:1-25, develops this theme still further and pictures these erstwhile enemies as being brought to acknowledge Yahweh's power. But that thought is not specifically expressed here.

In view of this type of usage it is perhaps inappropriate to add greatly to the very extensive discussion which has already taken

place concerning the precise location of the peoples here mentioned. "Ethiopia" (Heb. *kush*, rendered "Cush"), "Egypt," and
"Put" are linked at Gen. 10:6, but the "Libyans" (*lubim*) are not
referred to in any other biblical text earlier than 2 Chr. 12:3. An
additional complication arises from the fact that "Ethiopia" is
not coextensive with modern Ethiopia (Abyssinia); rather, it included much of the modern Sudan. "Put" may include Somalia.
Otherwise, it would appear that the reference is simply to different areas of modern Egypt, Libya, and the Sudan. In any case,
it seems that the names should be regarded as evocative of distant
and alien powers, rather than as precise geographical designations.

10   The fate of Thebes is described, with the implication that
Nineveh's fate will be at least as devastating. Once again we must
be careful to recognize that much of the language used is that
regularly applied to such circumstances, rather than a precise
description of what took place in Egypt. There is no reason, for
example, to suppose that this oracle reflects firsthand knowledge
of what took place in or immediately after 663.

With this in mind, we can see how the theme of being "carried
away . . . into captivity" is one that recurs in descriptions of this
kind. The present passage is particularly reminiscent of Isa. 20:4,
where it is asserted that "the king of Assyria [will] lead away the
Egyptians captives and the Ethiopians exiles." The fate of the
"little ones" is again all too familiar a feature of wartime atrocity.
But again there is a link with the Isaiah tradition which is worthy
of note: Isa. 13:16 uses exactly the same expression. It is noteworthy also that the somewhat unusual word for "honored men"
(*nikbad;* literally, "weighty ones") is also found in this sense at
Isa. 3:5 and 23:8. The most striking link with the last part of the
verse, however, is provided by Ps. 149:8:

> *to bind their kings with chains*
> *and their nobles with fetters of iron.*

Here the parallel is so close as to suggest either that this language
was regularly used in oracles against foreign nations or perhaps,
more specifically, that it may have been part of some liturgy
associated with holy war.

Attention is drawn to these links, not simply to stress the

literary as against the historical thrust of the book, but also to bring out what is sometimes left unexpressed in Nahum's own words and those of modern commentators. The parallels show that in all these threats and upheavals it is Yahweh who is completely in control; what is brought about is at his command and shows his sovereign power at work.

11 After the comparison with Thebes the poem reverts to direct address to Nineveh. In fact, the link between vv. 10 and 11 is closer than can easily be expressed in English, for the first two lines of each verse begin with the same Hebrew word, *gam*. Of this fourfold repetition only the first and third occurrences are rendered in English ("Yet," "also"), but the repetition effectively demonstrates that the fate of Thebes will also be that of Nineveh, its enemy.

The verse appears to be in the form of a curse, but the specific thrust is not easily identifiable, as is shown by the variety of modern translations. Where the RSV has "You will be drunken, you will be dazed," the NEB renders "You too shall hire yourself out, flaunting your sex." The first verb (*shakar*) normally means "to become drunk," but its metaphorical use is more naturally suited to victory than to abject defeat; and hence Godfrey Rolles Driver ("Linguistic and Textual Problems: Minor Prophets," *Journal of Theological Studies* 39 [1938]: 271) suggests reading *sakar* ("to hire oneself out"). It is an attractive suggestion, but probably the received text is acceptable. Confidence would more readily be achieved if the meaning of the second verb were established: the verb *'alam* ("to hide") gives none of the expected parallelism with the first verb. A variety of suggested understandings or emendations has been made, but the traditional view remains as likely as any, that the point being made relates to the city's imminent descent into obscurity.

12 The comparison made here is an unexpected one, found nowhere else in the OT. The fig tree is more often praised for its sweetness and good fruit (e.g., Judg. 9:11) than taken as a symbol of insecurity; but the text seems certain. Possibly an otherwise unknown proverbial expression is here being alluded to. One minor emendation which has often been proposed and may well be correct is to read *'am* for *'im*, with no consonantal changes.

"Your troops are first-ripe figs" gives better sense and parallelism than the rather weak "with first-ripe figs." (More extensive changes would be entirely speculative and seem unnecessary.)

13   To use the expression "like women" in a derogatory sense would not be acceptable today, but it is found several times in the OT (e.g., Isa. 19:16) as a dismissive way of referring to what had once been a powerful force. The ineffectiveness of the supposed human defenders of the city is matched by the way in which the material protection ("gates" and "bars") has also been rendered useless. The gates can no longer be closed against the enemy, and the wooden bars have been consumed by fire. It is possible to visualize something of the importance of the gates from the elaborate modern reconstructions of Assyrian gates in the British Museum in London.

14   The mockery continues, but now in a different literary form. Here the prophet speaks ironically, encouraging the defenders to engage in preparations to make themselves secure, even though he well knows how useless such efforts must inevitably be. So the first requirement of any besieged city is a water supply. Then, enemy attacks must be beaten off, and so the "forts" are to be strengthened. (The word "forts" here is the same as that translated "fortresses" in v. 12; the reason for the change in translation is not apparent.) Part of the irony lies in the fact that these supposed strong points will, when reduced by fire, become a threat instead of a protection.

The last three phrases are three staccato two-word commands in Hebrew, giving a vivid picture of urgent action in the besieged city. But we know that all such activity would be unavailing. Once again we find a link with the Isaiah tradition. At Isa. 41:25 the same expressions are used to depict the circumstances of defeat in war. The link is not clear in the RSV, which has emended one of the verbs in the Isaiah passage (reading "trample" instead of the verb here rendered "go"), but the juxtaposition of the same two verbs ("go"/"tread") and the same two nouns used as objects ("clay"/"mortar") is surely not accidental.

15   Once again in this verse the theme of destruction is set out by means of characteristic literary references rather than by anything that could be regarded as an attempt at an objective historical account. Three different modes of destruction are evoked, all of them widely used in the OT: fire, the sword, and the locust.

The relation of the two parts of this verse to each other is not entirely clear. The RSV, by introducing a double space into the middle of the verse, suggests that the attackers of Nineveh are being likened to the locust as an innumerable horde. But that makes an awkward transition to the following verses, and it is more likely that we should understand a concessive sense here: "[even though you] multiply yourselves like the locust." If that is so, the possibility must at least be borne in mind that the reference to the locust in the first half of the verse is a dittograph and should be deleted (so BHS); "fire" and "sword" are frequently found as a matching pair to describe total destruction.

No certainty exists as to the exact species of creature described by the two Hebrew words here used. The more common is '*arbeh*, here translated "grasshopper," but both this and *yeleq* as well as a number of similar terms are used widely in the OT to convey the sense of a destructive multitude (cf. Joel 1).

16 "You increased" should probably be emended (or perhaps understood without emendation) to read an imperative, with the same concessive sense that we have noted as likely in v. 15: "even though you. . . ." This particular theme is not developed further here; we are reminded of the taunt over Babylon in the book of Revelation, where much of that city's power is alleged to have come from trading (Rev. 18:11ff.).

The last part of this verse and v. 17 revert to the metaphor of the locust. The exact meaning and the sense within the context are not easily determined. The problem with meaning arises from uncertainty as to the force of the verb *pashat* (RSV "spreads its wings"). Some new stage of the locust's transformation seems to be implied (Brown-Driver-Briggs "strip off [the sheaths of its wings]"; cf. Koehler-Baumgartner), but more than that is not known. More important is the sense within the larger context. The NEB eases the problem by reversing the order of the two halves of the verse. BHS suggests that the last phrase ("the locust . . . flies away") is an addition, a view supported also by Keller, who regards this phrase as "certainly a gloss added by a learned reader" (Vuilleumier and Keller, *Michée, etc.*, 132). It may be so;

but it may also be that, in view of the rich interchange of figurative language in this part of the poem, the form we have is the
original.

17   The inadequacy of those very forces in which Nineveh had
put confidence continues to be the subject of the poem's mockery.
This whole theme of false trust is one very deeply rooted in the
prophetic tradition of the OT — most frequently in condemnations of the prophets' own people, but also, as here, against any
who dared to make claims concerning their own power. Here the
first Hebrew word, *minnezar*, is found nowhere else in the OT,
and its exact force is disputed: RSV "princes," NEB "secret
agents"; Koehler-Baumgartner, "guardsmen." It is most likely
that the word is a loanword from Assyrian, with the general sense
of "guard"; but it remains uncertain whether Nahum's use is
based on knowledge of the actual titles of Assyrian officials, as
suggested by A. S. van der Woude ("The Book of Nahum," 113),
or is simply another illustration of his wide-ranging command of
vocabulary.

Almost as rare is the word used in the second comparison,
taphsar, which is found elsewhere only in Jer. 51:27. The RSV
has "scribes" here, "marshals" in the Jeremiah passage. This
appears to be a word of Akkadian origin, and again the question
arises whether it is simply a reflection of the political situation
of the time of Nahum and Jeremiah, or whether it illustrates a
rich range of vocabulary. The word can properly be translated
as "scribes," though it almost certainly has military connotations
(Kevin J. Cathcart suggests "recruiting-officers" as the appropriate translation; *Nahum in the Light of Northwest Semitic*, 147-48).
In any case, the point of these comparisons is clear: military
might, even when at first sight it seems as destructive as a cloud
of locusts, is of no avail. The word for "locusts," a different one
from that found in vv. 15-16, is written twice in slightly variant
forms, either in error (dittography) or as a means of emphasis.

The remainder of the verse is relatively straightforward. The
habits of the locusts, affected by the rising sun, are comparable
to those of the forces in whom Nineveh trusts. "When the sun
rises, they fly away." It is perhaps not too fanciful to suggest that
the rising of the sun here is a deliberate allusion to the showing-
forth of Yahweh in his power. Such a comparison is found in the

Psalms (e.g., Ps. 19:5-6), and this would help to explain the unusual fact that the particular point of comparison with locusts should be their departure. Normally it is their dreaded arrival that evokes vivid comparisons within the OT; here the point would be that that power has been confronted by an even greater force.

Commentators differ as to whether the word translated "where" should be taken in this verse (as in the Hebrew verse division, followed by RSV) or as a question marking the beginning of the next part of the poem and so linked with the following words ("Where are your shepherds?"). The mocking tone would be well brought out by such an arrangement, but the symmetry of the poem is probably better preserved by the existing form.

18 "Shepherds" is a metaphor frequently used in the OT for rulers. Here presumably the reference is to the subordinate rulers set up by the Assyrian great king as his vicegerents. They are now as ineffective as those who sleep. The interjected phrase "O king of Assyria" has often been regarded as a later addition, but something of the kind is needed, since the forms of the word "your" in v. 17 were feminine and here they are masculine. This would correspond with the fact that the earlier references were to the city of Nineveh, while those here are to the king.

To obtain the reading "our nobles slumber," the verb *yishkenu*, normally "to dwell," is often emended to *yashenu* ("sleep"); the RSV may have done this, though no note is appended. On the other hand, there are a number of passages in the OT where the verb *shakan* has the sense of the sleep of death (cf. Isa. 26:19), and that may be the sense here. In any case, the main point is the ineffectiveness of those upon whom the king relies.

The word here translated "people" (*'am*) is the same as that rendered as "troops" in v. 13; the same translation would have been better here, for in both verses the sense is that of the ineffectiveness of the usual means of defense. More difficult is the word *naphoshu*, translated "are scattered." The word never occurs elsewhere with a comparable meaning, and so again we are confronted either with an error in transmission (a change to *naphotsu* would give the required sense) or with a further example of Nahum's unusually wide range of vocabulary.

19   The poem and the whole book conclude with the final assertion that there can be no turning back of the fate that is coming
upon Nineveh and its forces. Though this general sense is clear,
obscurities in detail remain to the end. In particular, the word
kehah ("assuaging") is found only here, and in effect the translation had to be deduced from the context. A final link with the
language of the Jerusalem cult is supplied by the reference to
clapping of hands; this is the expression used in Ps. 47:1 to denote
acknowledgment of God's sovereignty, particularly in the way in
which all who attempt to oppose him are overthrown. It is an
appropriate conclusion to the book of Nahum, the driving force
of which has been this confident assertion of God's supreme power.
Just as the "unceasing evil" of the oppressor has been universal
in its effects — "upon whom has [it] not come?" — so the realiza-
tion of God's power in the overthrow of that oppression will be
even more universal. (On the significance of the fact that the
book ends with a question, and the possible link with Jonah, see
above, pp. 12-13.)

EPILOGUE

The book of Nahum will never be the most widely read or the most popular part of the OT. Perhaps it will even continue, as it has in the past, to cause offense and embarrassment. Very often those who have wished to defend it have been reduced to claims about the quality of the poetry — claims which may be true enough but scarcely warrant biblical status. In fact, as this commentary has tried to show, there is more to be said. There is a message which is closely related to one of the great overarching themes of the OT. Nahum was convinced that God retained control, that he was still effective even though for the moment alien and hostile powers appeared to be triumphant. Themes expressed in Israel's cult, expressing confidence in the defeat of all that challenged God's ultimate power, were given wider and more lasting significance by being taken up into the prophetic collection and maintained as an essential element in the lasting faith of Israel.

BIBLIOGRAPHY

Commentaries

Maier, W. A. *The Book of Nahum* (St. Louis: Concordia, 1959).
Rudolph, W. *Micha – Nahum – Habakuk – Zephanja.* Kommentar zum Alten Testament (Gütersloh: Gerd Mohn, 1975).
Smith, J. M. P., W. H. Ward, and J. A. Bewer. *Micah, Zephaniah, Nahum, Habakkuk, Obadiah and Joel.* International Critical Commentary (Edinburgh: T. & T. Clark and New York: Scribners, 1911).
Vuilleumier, R., and C. A. Keller. *Michée, Nahoum, Habacuc, Sophonie.* Commentaire de l'Ancien Testament (Neuchatel: Delachaux et Niestlé, 1971).
Watts, J. D. W. *The Books of Joel, Obadiah, Jonah, Nahum, Habakkuk and Zephaniah.* Cambridge Bible Commentary (Cambridge and New York: Cambridge University Press, 1975).

Other Studies

Cathcart, K. J. *Nahum in the Light of Northwest Semitic.* Biblica et orientalia (Rome: Biblical Institute, 1973).
Christensen, D. L. *Transformations of the War Oracle in OT Prophecy* (Missoula: Scholars Press, 1975).
Eaton, J. H. *Vision in Worship: The Relation of Prophecy and Liturgy in the OT* (London: SPCK and New York: Seabury, 1981).
————, ed. *Readings in Biblical Hebrew* 2 (Birmingham: University of Birmingham, 1978).
Haldar, A. D. *Studies in the Book of Nahum.* Uppsala universitetsårskrift (Uppsala: Almqvist and Wiksell, 1947).
Jeremias, J. *Kulturprophetie und Gerichtsverkündigung in der späten Königszeit Israels.* Wissenschaftliche Monographien zum Alten und Neuen Testament (Neukirchen-Vluyn: Neukirchener Verlag, 1970).
Schulz, H. *Das Buch Nahum: Eine redaktionskritische Untersuchung.* Beihefte zur Zeitschrift für die alttestamentliche Wissenschaft (Berlin and New York: de Gruyter, 1973).

Articles

Christensen, D. L. "The Acrostic of Nahum Reconsidered," *Zeitschrift für die alttestamentliche Wissenschaft* 87 (1975): 17-30.

Coggins, R. J. "An Alternative Prophetic Tradition?" in *Israel's Prophetic Tradition*, ed. R. J. Coggins, A. Phillips, and M. A. Knibb (Cambridge and New York: Cambridge University Press, 1982), 77-94.

Dentan, R. C. "The Literary Affinities of Exodus XXXIV 6f," *Vetus Testamentum* 13 (1963): 34-51.

DeVries, S. J. "The Acrostic of Nahum in the Jerusalem Liturgy," *Vetus Testamentum* 16 (1966): 476-81.

Driver, G. R. "Farewell to Queen Huzzab!" *Journal of Theological Studies*, n.s. 15 (1964): 296-98.

————. "Linguistic and Textual Problems: Minor Prophets," *Journal of Theological Studies* 39 (1938): 260-73.

Glasson, T. F. "The Final Question in Nahum and Jonah," *Expository Times* 81 (1969): 54-55.

Gray, J. "The Hebrew Conception of the Kingship of God: Its Origin and Development," *Vetus Testamentum* 6 (1956): 268-85.

————. "The Kingship of God in the Prophets and Psalms," *Vetus Testamentum* 11 (1961): 1-29.

Muilenburg, J. "A Study in Hebrew Rhetoric: Repetition and Style," *Supplements to Vetus Testamentum* 1 (1953): 97-111.

Wiseman, D. J. "Nineveh," in *The Illustrated Bible Dictionary*, ed. J. D. Douglas and N. Hillyer (Leicester: Inter-Varsity and Wheaton: Tyndale, 1980) 2: 1089-92.

van der Woude, A. S. "The Book of Nahum: A Letter Written in Exile," *Oudtestamentische Studiën* 20 (1977): 108-26.

Other Works Cited

Brockington, L. H. *The Hebrew Text of the OT* (Oxford and New York: Oxford University Press, 1973).

Carroll, R. P. *From Chaos to Covenant: Prophecy in the Book of Jeremiah* (London: SCM and New York: Crossroad, 1981).

Childs, B. S. *The Book of Exodus*. Old Testament Library (Philadelphia: Westminster and London: SCM, 1974).

Greenberg, M. *Ezekiel 1 – 20*. Anchor Bible (Garden City, N.Y.: Doubleday, 1983).

Hayes, J. H., ed. *OT Form Criticism* (San Antonio: Trinity University Press, 1974).

Johnson, A. R. *The Cultic Prophet and Israel's Psalmody* (Cardiff: University of Wales, 1979).

————. *The Cultic Prophet in Ancient Israel*, 2nd ed. (Cardiff: University of Wales, 1979).

Swete, H. B. *An Introduction to the OT in Greek* (Cambridge: Cambridge University Press, 1900).

Vermes, G. *The Dead Sea Scrolls in English* (Harmondsworth and Baltimore: Penguin, 1962).

Vermeylen, J. *Du prophète Isaïe à l'apocalyptique*, 2 vols. Études Bibliques (Paris: Gabalda, 1977-78).

Whybray, R. N. *The Intellectual Tradition in the OT.* Beihefte zur Zeitschrift für die alttestamentliche Wissenschaft (Berlin and New York: de Gruyter, 1974).

JUDGMENT
BETWEEN
BROTHERS

A Commentary on the Book of
Obadiah

RICHARD J. COGGINS

CONTENTS

INTRODUCTION

1. OBADIAH AMONG THE PROPHETS

With Obadiah, as with Nahum, we are once again in the presence of one of the most neglected of OT books; and once again the reasons are not far to seek. Obadiah is the shortest book in the OT, a mere twenty-one verses. This little fragment is not accompanied by detailed information about the prophet after whom it is named, such as might provide the "personal interest" so much sought after in the 20th century. Indeed, even at the purely literary level, there is a limitation on the distinctiveness of Obadiah, since a large part of the book is found in only slightly variant form in Jer. 49, and there are also close links with Ezek. 25 and parts of Joel. We may conclude this brief catalogue of disadvantages by noting that the main content of Obadiah appears to be a scathing attack upon Judah's neighbor and frequent enemy, Edom. Even among the great prophets, Isaiah or Jeremiah or Amos, the oracles against foreign nations are usually those to which least attention is paid and those about which most embarrassment is felt. In all these ways, it seems as if Obadiah must have a negative verdict returned against it.

No suggestion will here be made that to understand all is to forgive all; but it is at least unlikely that we shall be able to appreciate a prophetic fragment of this kind without a greater measure of understanding, and so it is helpful to set out first what can legitimately be known about the book. At the very outset it should be borne in mind that it seems fruitless to attempt to understand it as anything other than part of a literary collection, the twelve Minor Prophets, among which it stands fourth in the normal order preserved in our Bibles. That is to say, nothing can be gained from any attempt to know the individual prophet or the date and circumstances in which he prophesied. The name

Obadiah is a common one, borne by about twelve different individuals in the OT; there are no grounds for identifying our prophet with any of the others so named. It is not even certain that it is a proper name here; since it means "servant of Yahweh" it is possible that this brief collection is an anonymous presentation of the views of what was regarded as a true "servant of Yahweh."

Since the main theme of the book is a condemnation of Edom, it is often assumed that the underlying historical circumstances can be reconstructed with some confidence. It seems clear that the overthrow of Judah and the destruction of Jerusalem by the armies of the Neo-Babylonian emperor Nebuchadnezzar in 597 B.C. and finally in 587/6 gave rise to a paying-off of old scores by Judah's enemies. Among its rivals of long standing was Edom. Curiously, at 2 Kgs. 24:2 various other neighboring states are mentioned, such as Moabites and Ammonites, but no mention is made there of Edom. However, at Ps. 137:7, which is commonly dated to the early years of the Exile, Edom is particularly singled out for vilification. These grounds together with the links between Obadiah and both Jeremiah and Ezekiel, each of whom was active in the 6th cent., have led to the widespread consensus that Obadiah should also be placed in that period. Additional support for anti-Edomite feelings at this period is sometimes claimed from the apocryphal book 1 Esdras. There it is asserted (1 Esdr. 4:45) that the Edomites were responsible for burning the Jerusalem temple. It is doubtful, however, whether this reference is based on independent historical information; more probably it is an interpretation based on Ps. 137 and Obadiah itself.

While such a dating must remain the most probable, it is wise to acknowledge that positive evidence in its support is virtually nonexistent. The argument is almost entirely a circular one: Edom is said to have done such-and-such things at this period, which helps to establish the date of Obadiah—only for it to emerge eventually that the only evidence for such actions comes from the book of Obadiah itself. Neither the generalized poetic reference in Ps. 137 nor the material in Jer. 49 can supply a genuine alternative line of evidence. The relation of Obadiah to Jer. 49 is too problematic to supply a historical setting.

It seems wise, therefore, to admit that there are no certain clues as to dating. The book contains a number of phrases that are commonly held to betray an origin in the Jerusalem cult, so that, as with Nahum, we shall need to consider whether or not Obadiah was a "cultic prophet." It is also clear that Edom is in a sense regarded here as a typical enemy. Not simply the empirical neighbor of Judah, but the enemy of Yahweh and his people, capable of all forms of wickedness — that is the final impression we gain after reading the attacks upon Edom. This is particularly clear in vv. 15-21, where a number of references to Edom are found; but the basic thrust is against "all the nations" (v. 15), every one of which will become "as though they had not been" (v. 16). Whether or not Obadiah had a specific cultic role, it is clear that such material could be used and reused and applied to a variety of the people's enemies.

It has sometimes been alleged that vv. 11-14 constitute an exception to this "timeless" quality, and that they refer to specific events. Otto Eissfeldt, for example, states quite categorically that "in vv. 11-14 . . . it is quite certain that there is reference to Edom's malicious attitude at the time of Jerusalem's destruction in 587" (*The OT: An Introduction*, 403). Eissfeldt argues further that these events must have been still fresh in mind. Even here, however, the highly stylized nature of the presentation urges caution. No one will dispute that these verses would be particularly appropriate in the time after 587, but we know too little of the detail of the history, or even whether the primary reference in Obadiah need necessarily be historical, to place these verses in that setting without further question. The problem is analogous to that of dating such a passage as Ps. 74, concerning which exactly the same arguments have been put forward.

2. PLACE

Once again there are no clear indications of the place of composition to be gleaned from the geographical allusions within the book; our only guide must be the literary usage. As will emerge in the Commentary, this is best understood as favoring Jerusalem. A number of passages seem likely to owe their origin to the language of the Jerusalem cult, though it may be freely admitted that the links here are less strong than they were with Nahum. If an exilic date is maintained, we should have to admit to insufficient knowledge of the condition of Jerusalem at that period to describe more precisely the circumstances in which the book might have taken shape. It is, perhaps, advisable to stress that there is no suggestion that the whole population of Jerusalem, still less that of Judah, was taken into exile. Though we have no details of the nature of continuing life after the final fall of Jerusalem, there is no ground for doubting that there was a continuing community, which would have engaged in understanding and explaining the disasters that had befallen it.

3. ISRAEL AND EDOM

Since for all practical purposes this little book is concerned with one single theme, it is important to set the scene for the Commentary by saying something more of what is known of relations between Israel and Edom. This is the more necessary in view of the curious ambivalence which runs through many of the references.

A number of OT passages speak of Edom as a brother to Israel (these are helpfully analyzed and discussed by J. R. Bartlett, "The Brotherhood of Edom," *Journal for the Study of the OT* 4 [1977]: 2-27). These passages may be listed as follows: a number of sections in Gen. 25, 27, 36; Num. 20:14-21; Deut. 2:4-8; 23:7; Jer. 49:7-11; Amos 1:11-12; Mal. 1:2-4, together, of course, with the material in Obadiah which is our immediate concern. It is not appropriate here to look at those passages in detail (for which purpose Bartlett's article may be commended), but two general issues are worthy of note. First, "brotherhood" by no means always implies an amicable relation. Thus, in Amos 1:11, if the "brother" for whose pursuit Edom is condemned is indeed Israel, as is very probable, there is no hint in the passage of any friendly relations between the two. Somewhat similar are those passages in Deut. 2 which imply a relation between Israel and Edom as a basis for Israel's appeal for safe conduct at the time of their passage toward the promised land, but the plea goes unanswered by Edom. Second, it appears as if the presentation of Israel and Edom as "brothers" is in some way related to the presentation in Genesis of Jacob and Esau as brothers. Simply to state this does little to resolve the problem of the nature of the relationship. It is impossible to treat as strict history the idea that Jacob and Esau were literally the founders of the two nations, all of whose people were descended from them. The relation between the stories of individuals in Genesis and the later "brotherhood" of nations is a complex one, not least because of the geographical shift that has taken place. Edom was in the far south, whereas the stories of Jacob and Esau place their activities in central Transjordan. The Genesis stories already give some indication of a more complex development by the inclusion of such notes as Gen. 25:30b ("Therefore his name was called Edom"), which indicates both a wordplay in the Hebrew and also a link with the later nation of that name.

In view of these uncertainties it is not surprising that there is no agreement among scholars whether there was some particular historical development which led to this identification of two groups as "brothers" or whether the presentation is a purely literary one. The same uncertainty arises when we consider such passages as Deut. 23:7 which imply a more favorable view of Edom than of other neighbors. Again, it is possible that some historical fact, such as an alliance involving both nations, underlay this presentation; or it may be that once again a purely literary development is implied.

Bearing all these difficulties in mind, we can be confident only in saying that there is clear evidence of hostility between Judah and Edom from the time of David, around 1000 B.C. (2 Sam. 8:13-14, accepting with RSV and NEB the emendation "Edomites" in v. 13 for MT "Aramaeans"), and possibly from the time of Saul (1 Sam. 14:47), right through the monarchical period. Presumably the periodic wars between Judah and Edom were interspersed with intervals of reconciliation, though as has just been seen it would go beyond the evidence to link such intervals with the more favorable passages such as Deut. 23:7. From the 6th cent. onward, the time of Babylonian and then Persian ascendancy, neither Judah nor Edom was able for any extended period to regain its former identity as a nation-state. Judah was incorporated into the imperial provincial system, and the great powers exercised a general hegemony over Edom.

Edom was, however, more remote from the main trade routes and less involved in the ebb and flow of political events. Any advantage which this might have produced was, however, short-lived. The old Edomite territory came under increasing pressure from different Arab groups, notably the Nabataeans, who by the last centuries B.C. had driven out much of the old Edomite stock. This group in turn established itself in southern Palestine, the area which came to be known as Idumaea (from the name Edom). To the OT writers, including Obadiah, such incursions were an invasion of the sacred territory, the promised land, for which the Edomites ought properly to be condemned. From our very different modern standpoint we might suppose that the Edomites had no option in the matter, as they found themselves under increasing pressure from the invading Arabs. (We need not agree with the viewpoint expressed in the book of Obadiah, but it is important to try to understand it if we are to come to any appreciation of the book.)

Nothing more need be said here about the history, which is in any case obscure and cannot affect our understanding of the book of Obadiah. It is, however, worth noting that Herod the Great, who is referred to in the birth narratives of Jesus, was described as an Idumaean. Almost certainly this description can be taken as factually accurate, though it is not impossible, given the hostility of many Jewish groups to Herod and all that he stood for, that this was more a term of abuse than an accurate account of his origins.

4. LITERARY RELATIONSHIPS

Some consideration must now be given to the literary problems which Obadiah poses. These fall broadly into two categories. There is, first, the question of the unity of the oracles. Despite the brevity of the book there have not been wanting critics who have proposed to see several literary strata within the material which has come down to us. (Leslie C. Allen gives a useful analysis of the different types of view held on this matter; *Joel, etc.*, 133-36.) The detection of such strata may be legitimate, but it is worth noting that the likely cultic origin of the material may be relevant here. We know too little of the organization of material within a cultic context to be confident in any precise literary analysis. It is indeed probable that the material is diverse in origin, but in its present form it has been drawn together into one unified whole. The second question cannot be dismissed so briefly. It concerns the relation between Obadiah and other prophetic material, notably Jer. 49. Jeremiah 49 forms part of that block of material, differently placed in the Hebrew and Greek forms of that book, which comprises oracles against foreign nations. Though some elements in that collection may go back to Jeremiah himself, it is noteworthy that there are few pointers in these chapters to a specific, identifiable context, either in Jeremiah's own ministry or in the history of his time. Rather, the links which can be traced are for the most part with other blocks of oracles against foreign nations in the prophets. We have already seen some links of this kind with Nahum, and there are others between Jer. 46 – 51 and Isa. 13 – 23.

This being the case, it would probably be an oversimplification to envisage a direct dependence of either Obadiah on Jeremiah or of Jeremiah on Obadiah, though in the past many commentators have done so. It is more probable that each prophetic collection was drawing upon and using for its own purposes a common stock of material, whose origin should probably be sought in a cultic context (that is, in the people's heritage of worship), in which Yahweh was proclaimed as the mighty warrior who might punish both his enemies and his own people. (This point is discussed more fully below, pp. 74-76.)

The main parallels with Jer. 49 are as follows:

With Obad. 1a   compare Jer. 49:7
            1b-4   49:14-16
            5-6   49:9-10a

As will be indicated in the Commentary, these links are of varying degrees of closeness. In the remainder of Obadiah there are also similarities with Jer. 49, though not of so detailed a kind: in particular, v. 8 may be compared with Jer. 49:7, v. 9 with Jer. 49:22b, and v. 16 with Jer. 49:12.

There are also links with other prophetic collections, in particular with Joel, another brief prophetic book about whose date and circumstances of origin there is no certainty. Joel 2:32 includes the expression "in Mount Zion and in Jerusalem there shall be those who escape, as the LORD has said"; the latter phrase could be an indication that Joel is later and acknowledges the authority of the prophetic words in Obadiah in the context of an actual quotation. It may be so; but perhaps here and elsewhere Obadiah and Joel are drawing upon a collection of oracular material in a way analogous to what we have seen probably to be the case with Obadiah and Jer. 49.

Other links between Obadiah and Joel may also be noted: Obad. 11 and Joel 3:3; v. 15 and Joel 1:15; v. 16 and Joel 3:17; v. 18 and Joel 2:5. Some of these links are no more than turns of phrase which may be coincidental (and in some cases they are not very clearly illustrated by the English translation). Nevertheless, so many similarities in two short books reinforce the conclusion that there was a store of vocabulary, probably of Jerusalemite origin, upon which different prophetic collections might draw. The links with Joel are especially striking insofar as Joel contains no anti-Edomite polemic. From this it would appear that Obadiah was using phraseology that might be given a variety of interpretations and was applying it specifically to Edom.

We may notice finally that another prophetic book, Ezekiel, also includes a section of oracles against foreign nations, among them a brief oracle against Edom (Ezek. 25:12-14). Though the links with Obadiah are much less close than those to be found in Jer. 49, there is again a shared use of characteristic phraseology which reminds us once more of the very close links holding together the foreign nations material in the different prophetic books.

5. THEOLOGY

Such a heading may cause some surprise. One recent introduction has stated flatly that Obadiah "is of little theological interest" (J. A. Soggin, *Introduction to the OT,* 341). Such a dismissive judgment may, however, need some modification.

The literature of the OT, at least from the time of the Exile onward, is consistent with the portrayal of Yahweh as a God who has entered into a unique relation with a particular people. That relation is projected back to the earliest existence of the people, and is characterized in particular by the conviction that Yahweh had brought his people to a promised land, the land "flowing with milk and honey." A corollary of such an understanding of God and his dealings with his people was a conviction that Israel was to be sharply differentiated from other peoples, and was indeed to engage in war with them (or, better, to act as Yahweh's instruments when *he* waged war against them). An important feature of Israel's religious practice was, therefore, an invocation of God against all enemies who encroached on the privileges, and in particular on the land, which God had given to his people.

Such an understanding of God and his dealings with his people carried with it the belief that, if God were displeased with his people he might punish them, just as he would punish other countries which offended against him. A number of consequences follow from this pattern of belief and practice. First, though Israel was in a special relation with God, there is an implicit assumption running throughout the prophetic books that other nations too have certain standards of behavior laid down to which they must conform or risk punishment. Such standards have sometimes been called "natural law," but that expression comes from a different cultural background and may not be helpful in understanding the OT. Better, we should simply note that there were certain forms of behavior which were unacceptable and, it was believed, *were known to be so* by all nations.

Second, the OT (and, indeed, the NT) comes from an age when war was simply a fact of life. No difficulty was felt in using the idea of war in quite an unselfconscious way in mapping out an understanding of God's action. God was pictured as a king, and one of the characteristic actions of kings was to go to war (2 Sam. 11:1). For at least two reasons such an understanding is particularly difficult to accept in the 20th century. The threat of nuclear war has brought with it a total reappraisal of the place of warfare, so that the whole idea of a "just war" is now widely regarded as a thing of the past. More generally, death is now a fact which members of advanced societies tend to remove completely from their vision; and warfare means death. Death was treated in a much more matter-of-fact way in the OT, and so the idea of warfare (with the inevitability of death) was again something which could more readily be envisaged.

These considerations are relevant to many parts of the OT. A third point is more specifically applicable to Obadiah. In the early oracles against foreign nations, for example those in Amos, it seems clear that a specific identifiable enemy is being addressed. We may not now be able to reconstruct the precise historical circumstances in each case, but we feel that they could be reconstructed if more information on the history of the period were to become available. In the later OT books, and still more

in the postbiblical apocalypses, God's enemies are no longer identifiable as empirical nations; they have become symbolic of all
that is evil and opposed to God's plans.

In that development Obadiah represents a particular stage.
His oracles are clearly aimed against Edom; yet at several points,
as will be noted in the Commentary, it is not just that particular
nation, carrying out specific unacceptable acts, which is the tar-
get of condemnation; Edom is becoming a symbol of all that
stands in enmity to God. In theological terms, this is an illustration of a dilemma which is constantly arising. It may be readily
accepted that evil is to be resisted, fought against with all the
weapons that are available. But difficulty arises when, as is inevitable, that evil has to be associated with a particular group of
people who are also properly to be seen as God's creatures. There
is no ready solution to this problem, and it is certainly not re-
solved in the book of Obadiah. Nevertheless, the book of Obadiah
does provide important clues for our reflection when confronted
with such a tension. Theologically, then, it may be right to say
of Obadiah that, even if none of the heights of other parts of the
OT are reached, we are nevertheless confronted with basic and
familiar problems which still haunt us today; and if no tidy an-
swers are provided, at least the dimensions of the struggle against
evil are clearly delineated.

COMMENTARY

1 The collection is described, as was the book of Nahum, as a "vision." As we saw when commenting on Nah. 1:1, no differentiation in modern terms is possible between those experiences which speak of "words" and those which use the imagery of sight. Perhaps the clearest illustration of this is found in Ps. 89:19: "thou didst *speak* in a *vision* to thy faithful one."

We have already noted that "Obadiah" was a common name in the OT. We have no means of knowing whether the name here (which is not found again in the book) is based on a known prophetic figure, who was regarded — rightly or wrongly — as the originator of these words, or whether these words were thought to be especially appropriate for a "servant of Yahweh" in their denunciation of foreign wickedness.

The oracular section of the book introduces us at once to the links with Jer. 49, to which reference has already been made. The oracles against foreign nations in Jer. 46–51 are regularly introduced with the phrase "concerning X"; the phrase "concerning Edom" at Obad. 1 is also found in Jer. 49:7. Whereas in Nahum we saw that there has been disagreement whether the material had originally been directed against Nineveh or only secondarily reapplied in that sense, here it is almost universally assumed that this particular block of material has been anti-Edomite from its origin. This may be so, but we shall need to note that many phrases could be of more general application.

The imagery of the remainder of the verse (plural here, singular in Jer. 49:14) is probably derived from the idea of the divine council. God is often pictured in the OT as a king, and one obvious characteristic of kings is that they have courtiers: lesser beings who can advise the ruler, carry out royal commissions, and help in planning the good order of the kingdom. (Job 1 provides a well-known example of a discussion within the divine

77

council.) In prophetic oracles a frequently used figure of speech is to envisage the prophet as having been summoned into that council to be told what plans God had in mind and to play his part as a messenger in making them more widely known and implementing them. (This is vividly illustrated by the story of Micaiah in 1 Kgs. 22, esp. vv. 19-23.) In Obadiah the divine council has been deliberating and has decided to prepare for battle — again a characteristic activity of kings in the ancient world.

Two important theological points are brought out by the fact that the summons to war has been sent by a messenger "among the nations." First, we see once more, as in Nahum, that in the ancient world war was an acceptable image to use of God's activity. It is still so in the NT, where Jesus is presented as speaking about warfare between kings as an everyday occurrence which can form the basis of a parable (Luke 14:31), and the Epistle to the Ephesians likens the Christian duty to the wearing of military armor (Eph. 6:10-20). Christian hymnody, too, is full of warlike language which poses one of the most acute problems of reinterpretation facing the Church in a century of "total war."

Second, we see in the manner in which the nations are here summoned a transformation in prophetic attitudes toward other peoples. Those nations will wage war against Edom, supposing that they are doing so at their own whim and for their own advantage. In fact, their decision is not their own but the LORD'S. Just as in Isa. 10:5-15 Assyria was no more than the rod in Yahweh's hand, though supposing that its own power had brought it victory, so here the nations are pictured as being under the control of Israel's God.

2 "I will make you small." The verb is a perfect, which (at least in prose) normally denotes a past tense, and it was so translated by older versions (e.g., RV). But the RSV is surely right in taking it as a future, perhaps the so-called prophetic perfect, stressing the inevitability of what is announced. The significance of "small" and "despised" here will be brought out through the contrast with Edom's own pretensions expressed in the next verse.

3 This verse combines a motif applied very widely in oracles against foreign nations with a theme peculiar to Edom. It is

characteristic of the condemnations of foreign nations to draw
attention to their false boasting (cf. Isa. 10:5-15 or the boasts of
the Philistine giant in 1 Sam. 17), and that is the significance of
the condemnation of "pride" here. The same expression is used
in condemning Babylon at Jer. 50:31-32: "I am against you, O
proud one. . . . The proud one shall stumble and fall."

But this more generally applicable theme could be applied to
Edom with particular aptness because of the notorious nature of
that region's terrain. "The clefts of the rock" is the RSV translation of the Hebrew phrase *hagwe-sela'*. The word *sela'* can mean
rocky places in general. But it is likely that there is a more specific
reference here, as noted in the RSV margin, to a place called
Sela', which had been captured in the 8th cent. by Judah (2 Kgs.
14:7) and was one of the chief Edomite cities (see J. R. Bartlett,
"The Moabites and the Edomites," in D. J. Wiseman, ed., *Peoples of OT Times*, esp. 237 and n. 55). The common identification of Sela' with Petra, the famous "rose-red city, half as old as
time" of John William Burgon's poem, though attractive, cannot
be confidently established for lack of adequate evidence.

The verse ends with another form characteristic of oracles
directed against the arrogance of foreign nations. Those nations
are represented as putting what *they* take to be a rhetorical question: "Who will bring me down to the ground?" They suppose
that there is no one who could do so. The prophet implies that
there is a very direct answer to such a question: Yahweh will
bring them down! (A similar use of this form is found at Isa.
10:11.)

4   This point is explicitly asserted in the words "I will bring you
down, says the LORD" — despite all false pretensions. These four
opening verses have clearly established the basic theme of the
book: the effectiveness of Yahweh's power is asserted despite all
false claims to sovereignty. If, as is commonly supposed, Obadiah
was composed during the Exile, with Jerusalem in ruins and the
temple destroyed, this is a remarkable assertion. It may have
been a traditional form taken over from the cult; but even cultic
forms, conservative though they tend to be, do develop in accordance with changing historical circumstances. It seems as if here
we are seeing one stage in the development toward the kind of
theology of history expressed, for example, in the Deuterono-

mistic history, according to which all that had befallen Israel was attributable to the act of Yahweh.

5 The imagery of this verse is found also in Jer. 49:9, though the actual arrangement of the strophes differs markedly. "Thieves" and "plunderers" are synonyms here (both words should be retained, as against BHS, which proposes deleting "plunderers" as a gloss), though elsewhere the nuances of the words differ. "Thieves" are those who work in secret; "plunderers" might well use violence. This metaphor of destruction being likened to the work of "thieves" and "plunderers" may find its first OT usage here; it is found in the NT in relation to the expected coming of the LORD (1 Thess. 5:2; cf. John 10:1-10). The Hebrew word *eyk* ("How") may have originated as a mourning cry, as in David's lament over Saul and Jonathan, "How are the mighty fallen!" (2 Sam. 1:19). Here its use is clearly ironic; the mourning cry has become a shout of jubilation at the downfall of the proud enemy.

The exact force of the next phrase (RSV "would they not steal only enough for themselves?") is not clear. It seems again to be a question in mocking form, which could be translated literally, "Will they not steal their sufficiency?" The RSV's version is one possibility, in which case the implication would be that whereas thieves take only as much as they need, the inevitable destruction of Edom will be even worse than the devastation caused by thieves. But this may be to take too rosy a view of the damage done by thieves, and it is perhaps more likely that the totality of the destruction brought about by thieves is in mind. The JB translation brings out the point well.

> *If robbers came to you,*
> *or plunderers at night,*
> *they would steal to their heart's content.*
> *If grape-gatherers came to you,*
> *they would leave no gleanings behind them.*

A marginal note explains the point, that Edom's despoliation is more thorough than usual.

6 Whereas v. 5 is very close to Jer. 49:9, this verse is only distantly related to 49:10. In the text as it stands the only direct link is by the use of the name "Esau" for Edom. There is, however, another similarity whose precise significance is difficult to evaluate. In Jeremiah the verse begins "I have stripped Esau bare," the Hebrew verb being *hasaph;* here in Obadiah, "How Esau has been pillaged," the verb is the very similar one *haphas.* The visual similarity of the two verbs does not extend to likeness of meaning, and it would be altogether too tidy a solution to propose that either should be emended to conform to the other. Nevertheless, it does seem likely that the two forms are deliberately reminiscent of each other.

The use of the proper name "Esau" at once calls to mind the Genesis stories. Often in the OT when the proper name is used it appears as if some specific characteristic associated with Esau in Genesis is being recalled, as for example at Mal. 1:2-3. Here and in the later uses of the name in Obadiah it is difficult to discern any such allusion, and it seems as if Esau is simply an alternative form of Edom. This is the same ambiguity as is found in Gen. 25:30 and ch. 36.

7 Thematically this verse corresponds with Jer. 49:10b, which also makes the point of the unreliability of human attachments; but there is no direct association of vocabulary between the two verses. Once again the question arises whether some particular historical episode underlies this taunt, or whether a literary basis should be sought. The latter seems more probable, though this may be simply the result of our ignorance of the historical background of Obadiah. It does seem, however, that the most plausible way of understanding this verse is by likening it to a form commonly found in individual psalms of lament, where the psalmist bemoans the way in which he has been deserted by those who should have been his closest supporters. Psalm 41:9 and 55:12-15 provide vivid examples. But whereas in the Psalms the supplicant is ruing his own fate, here that fate is pictured as having befallen the Edomites. The expressions translated "your allies" and "your confederates" may have a religious rather than a historical-political meaning. In particular, a literal rendering of the first phrase would be "men of your covenant"; if Obadiah is rightly dated in the exilic period or a little later, this was a time when the idea of God's covenant with his people played an important part in prophetic preaching (cf. Jer. 31; Ezek. 36). By contrast with the true covenant between Yahweh and his people, no other covenant could stand.

The last part of the verse presents considerable difficulties in interpretation. The Hebrew text contains the word *lahmeka* ("your bread"), whose meaning in the context is not at all clear. The RSV translation "your trusted friends" sets the expression in parallel with the "allies" and "confederates" of the earlier part of the verse; this meaning is probably arrived at by pursuing further the parallel already noted with the psalms of lamentation. Thus at Ps. 41:9 the false friend is described as the one who "ate of my bread," and something of the same kind is probable here. (Leslie C. Allen lists earlier scholars who have taken this or a substantially similar view; *Joel, etc.*, 150.) If this is not the sense, then we must say that the original force of the verse is now irrecoverable.

A difficulty of a different kind arises from the word *mazor*, which occurs nowhere else in the Hebrew Bible. The RSV translation "trap" is in effect determined by the context, which requires some such sense, and is the meaning found in the ancient versions; whether there is any corruption in the Hebrew form we cannot tell.

Theologically more important is the transition signified at the end of the verse to a new theme, that of wisdom. The phrase "there is no understanding of it" fits somewhat awkwardly with what has gone before, and some commentators (e.g., H. W. Wolff; cf. also BHS) have taken it to be a gloss. Even if it is accepted as an integral part of the verse, there is no agreement as to the referent of the final "it." The most likely explanations are either that the reference is to the "trap," which catches its victim unawares — that is, with "no understanding"; or it might be to Edom, in which case it would be better to translate "there is no understanding *in* it," the phrase being understood as an introduction to the next verse. This latter suggestion seems the more satisfactory solution, and may be accepted whether or not the phrase be a later addition.

8 Whatever is to be said of the last phrase of v. 7, there can be no question that the theme of this verse is Edomite wisdom. As noted already, there is a link in content with Jer. 49:7, though in this case there is no question of literary dependence: the verses simply have in common the certain overthrow of any claims to wisdom made by the Edomites. There are no other unambiguous references to Edomite wisdom in the OT; Baruch 3:22 (in the Apocrypha) may be regarded as an independent tradition, but some scholars have nevertheless argued that these verses supply sufficient evidence for us to be able to speak of a strongly established wisdom tradition in Edom. Robert H. Pfeiffer, for example, proposed an Edomite origin for the book of Job on this basis (*Introduction to the OT,* 680-83). It seems unlikely that there is sufficient evidence to establish this kind of conclusion (see Bartlett, "The Moabites and Edomites," 246-47); rather it may be that the mockery here is akin to that noted in the preceding verse. Claims to true wisdom outside Israel are derided as being useless, comparable to the false claims to competence and expertise which could in fact only lead to disaster, as we have seen already in vv. 3-4. It would seem, therefore, that we should be cautious about making too precise judgments about Edomite wisdom; the famous assessment of Solomon that his "wisdom surpassed the wisdom of all the people of the east" (1 Kgs. 4:30) makes no specific reference to Edom. In short, this passage is best seen as a warning against excess of ambition.

"Mount Esau" is an unexpected phrase, found only in the book of Obadiah. Once again, it is probable that the idea is theological rather than geographical, with the reference being to the height of false claims rather than to any specific location. Certainly, if a link with the Esau of Genesis is intended it is difficult to envisage that he would be associated with a mountain so far distant from the Transjordanian home of the Esau traditions.

9 The interpretation given to Edomite wisdom in the previous verse finds further support here. The "wise men" of v. 8 are not to be taken out of context; rather, they are to be seen in parallel with the "mighty men" here. Once again we have a warning against hubris or human insolence; all who trust in human military might will themselves be slaughtered. There is, of course, no suggestion here or elsewhere that Edom was especially noted for "mighty men."

"Teman" is referred to on a number of occasions in the OT. It may have been the name of a city; modern Tawilân, near Petra, has been proposed as its site. More frequently, however, it seems to be either the name of a district of Edom, as in Amos 1:12 where "Teman" and "Bozrah" are the two districts of which Edom is composed, or an alternative way of describing the whole area. The latter view is the usage here, where "Teman" is synonymous with "Mount Esau" as a description of Edom. (At Gen. 36:11 Teman is found as a personal name, but that poses problems which are outside our present concern.)

More interesting is the fact that at Hab. 3:3 we find "God came from Teman, and the Holy One from Mount Paran" in a context which makes it clear that it is Yahweh, the God of Israel, to whom reference is being made. Here we find expressed once again, and in a strikingly different way, the tradition of the close links between Israel and Edom implicit in the "brotherhood" stories of Jacob and Esau.

The Hebrew text, followed by the RSV, has the word "slaughter" at the end of this verse, whereas the ancient versions for the most part linked it with the following verse. Both placings have been supported by modern commentators, as has a third, perhaps more likely, suggestion that this is a gloss upon, or an alternative to, the word "violence" in v. 10.

10   With v. 10 we reach a new section of the book in two senses. First, at the literary level, the detailed links with Jer. 49 are now at an end (the thematic link between v. 16 and Jer. 49:12 is only a very partial exception to this claim). Second, there is a change of theme. From the announcement of doom upon Edom the emphasis now turns to a spelling out of the wrongs which have made such a doom inevitable. The poetic structure of the book is not sufficiently clear, nor is there enough agreement among scholars as to the determinative characteristics of Hebrew poetry, for a confident judgment to be reached as to whether the poetic arrangement reflects a similar division (see Allen, *Joel, etc.*, 140-42 for a discussion of some of the commonly held views).

What is "the violence done to your brother Jacob"? If it was some contemporary atrocity, as the urgent language of this section has led some scholars to suppose, then we have to confess that we are ignorant of what it may have been. Verse 11 might appear to point to a particular time when Judah had been overrun by enemies, but it is doubtful whether the two verses should be so closely linked as to allow the interpretation of one to shape that of the other. Here the charge is "violence"; in v. 11 it is a very different matter: "you stood aloof." It seems more likely that we have here an example of the reuse of a frequently repeated and almost stereotyped accusation against Edom, which is placed in a particular historical context at Num. 20:20-21 and is picked up again in Judg. 11:17 and possibly in Amos 1:11. The description of Israel as "Jacob" here also serves as an allusion back to the patriarchal stories, as does the designation of Edom in the preceding verses as "Esau."

The assertion that the impending punishment will be "for ever" is characteristic of the prophetic oracles against foreign nations (cf. Isa. 14:20), and provides an important link to the modes of thought and expressions characteristic of the later apocalypses. In these Yahweh's eternal power, wielded against his enemies, is a basic theme; this is especially characteristic of many of the postbiblical apocalypses, e.g., 1 En. 91. The use of this motif against Edom is found also in Ezek. 35:9, "I will make you a perpetual desolation," where the word *'olam* ("perpetual") is practically identical with the form here rendered "for ever."

11 The governing theme of the next few verses is that of the "day." Hebrew *yom* ("day") occurs at least once in each verse and eleven times in all in vv. 11-15, and in the present form of the text (there is dispute, as we shall see, whether v. 15a has been displaced) the climax is reached with the announcement in v. 15 that this day is "the day of the LORD."

Here, as elsewhere in Obadiah and more generally in the OT, there is a complex relationship between historical and theological assertions. The theme of the day of the LORD is characteristically that of judgment; it is a day when God brings judgment upon all who have fallen short of the demands made upon them. Characteristically, those victims of judgment will be the enemies of Israel; but on a number of occasions the prophets warn that Israel itself will not be immune from the threat of judgment. The frequency with which similar phrases and motifs are found suggests that the background of this language was cultic. But such a background should not lead us to suppose that historical events had no part to play in the building up of this picture of the day. Judgment was given, to some extent at least, on the basis of specific wrong acts, and it is most likely that one occasion for the gathering together of the book of Obadiah was the conviction that Edom had, by such specific wrong acts, transgressed the will of Yahweh and would be the victim of judgment at his day. Some such understanding seems essential to make good sense of the verses which here follow, gradually building up to their climax in v. 15.

At the outset it appears as if the historical reference is uppermost. Some specific event has taken place in which the Edomites were held to have forgotten any ties of brotherhood and had "stood aloof" at the time of Jerusalem's need. As Wolff notes (*Dodekapropheten 3: Obadja und Jona*, 18), the adverbial expression here translated "aloof" signifies both distance and opposition. If a historical occasion is sought, it is most natural to suppose that the reference must be to the destruction of Jerusalem at Babylonian hands in 587/6. Such a historical "day" of failure would meet its consequence in the inevitable "day" to which the prophet now looks forward.

Even in this verse, apparently concerned as it is with past events, it is noteworthy that some of the phrases used are stereotyped expressions regularly found in the accounts of enemy assaults upon the holy city. Such accounts commonly develop one of two themes; either they proclaim Yahweh's power over his enemies, whose assaults are doomed to failure thereby, or they implore Yahweh to reassert himself because of his apparent inactivity. Joel 3:1-3 is an example of the first type, announcing the inevitable destruction of "all the nations"; Ps. 74:4-11 is of the second type, a lament imploring God to act on behalf of his stricken people.

The expression, "and cast lots for Jerusalem," found also in Nah. 3:10 where it was used in the description of the fate of Nineveh, is a characteristic way of describing the division of a victim's spoils by his conqueror. It is again part of the imagery found in psalms of lament, the most famous example being Ps. 22:18, which is specifically quoted in John 19:24 and alluded to in the other Gospel passion narratives as being fulfilled in the passion of Jesus.

One other noteworthy point in this verse is the way in which it illustrates the interchangeability of place and personal names in a context such as this. Just as "Edom" had been referred to sometimes as Esau, a personal name, and sometimes as "Teman," a place name, so after the reference to the personal name "Jacob" in the previous verse we now find the use of "Jerusalem" here. This use is all the more remarkable in that the casting of the lots in the other examples cited always had a personal reference. Perhaps it is not irrelevant in this connection to note that the Hebrew words for "humanity" and "land" (*adam* and *adamah*) are very closely akin to one another.

12   One of the most clearly defined subunits of the whole book embraces vv. 12-14. It is a series of prohibitions, each beginning in the same Hebrew form (*we'al* + verb) and ending with the phrase "in the day of. . . ." The words qualifying "day of" all denote some form of distress; it is disputed whether those cases where the same form is found twice ("distress," vv. 12 and 14) or three times ("calamity," v. 13) represent secondary expansion or are a deliberate repetition for effect.

There is difficulty, too, in knowing how best to translate the opening prohibitions. The RV, with its series of prohibitions ("look not" . . . "rejoice not"), has retained the Hebrew form, but perhaps at the expense of the true sense. The RSV, with its series of "you should not have . . ." clauses, has abandoned the original form but may be nearer to the sense, provided that we do not take what follows simply as a statement of unadorned historical facts. Series of prohibitions of this kind are found both in the prophetic and in the wisdom literature, but no other example builds up the rhetorical effect in the same measure as this passage with its eightfold repetition.

If, as has already been suggested, the "day" referred to in the series of warnings was Jerusalem's devastation at the hands of the Babylonians, a link may be noted with Ps. 137. That psalm also laments the fall of Jerusalem and at v. 7 uses the expression "the day of Jerusalem." There, it is alleged, the Edomites had cried

> *"Rase it, rase it!*
> *Down to its foundations!"*

At Obad. 12, in a comparable way, they "gloated . . . rejoiced . . . boasted" over its downfall. The theme of Edomite pride, already adumbrated in v. 3, is thus developed and made more specific.

13   "The LORD loves the gates of Zion," sang the psalmist (Ps. 87:2); and frequently in the Psalms those gates are treated as symbolizing in a unique way the LORD'S presence with his people (cf. 9:14; 118:20). It is therefore natural that we should find in the laments the conviction that, just as the gates had symbolized God's presence, so their destruction was a sign of the withdrawal of that divine presence. The gates, supposedly inviolable, had been breached; God was angry with his people.

> *The kings of the earth did not believe,*
> *or any of the inhabitants of the world,*
> *that foe or enemy could enter*
> *the gates of Jerusalem.*
> *This was for the sins of her prophets*
> *and the iniquities of her priests.* (Lam. 4:12-13)

In those verses the lament acknowledges that the leaders of the people were themselves responsible for God's anger and for the punishment that had been inflicted as a result. Here in Obadiah the reaction is different; it is to blame the heathen nations who had been instrumental in carrying out the punishment. To "have entered the gate of my people" is part of the offense of the Edomites.

The other characteristic feature of this verse is a wordplay of the kind beloved by Hebrew poets, which inevitably is lost in translation. The word translated "calamity" in the RSV is in Hebrew *edam* in its first occurrence and *edo* in the other two; here there is clearly a wordplay with "Edom." It may not be taking the thought of the oracle too far to see in it the suggestion that what had appeared as a "calamity" for Israel would ultimately prove to be a calamity for the Edomites themselves, because of their failure to side with their brother in the time of his distress.

14   The series of accusations ends by listing two further offenses of the Edomites against their neighbors. Unfortunately, the sense of the first line is not clear; the Hebrew word *pereq,* here translated "parting of the ways," occurs elsewhere in the Hebrew Bible only at Nah. 3:1, where it is translated "booty," a sense demanded by the context there. Perhaps some sense of parting or tearing apart will provide an adequate basis for the two meanings (so Allen, *Joel, etc.,* 159); alternatively it may be the case that the two words, though identical in form, are in fact unrelated in meaning.

The remainder of the verse, with its reference to "fugitives" and "survivors," brings out vividly the horrors of war as experienced by the population of the nation which has suffered defeat. These lines also supply at the literary level a link back to vv. 9-10. Here the Edomites had "cut off his [Israel's] fugitives"; at vv. 9-10 Edom itself would be cut off "by slaughter . . . for ever."

15   The major break within the book of Obadiah occurs at this point. Though there are obvious thematic links between the two parts, there is also a marked new development away from the direct concern with contemporary Edom toward an eschatological picture of the destruction of "all the nations." Many scholars have regarded the remaining verses as additions from another hand (Allen offers a survey of scholarship; *Joel, etc.,* 133-36). Such a view should certainly not be dismissed, but it is doubtful whether so short a collection of oracles offers enough criteria for confident decision on this point. While there is clearly a change of emphasis, there is no obvious difference in literary style, and it has been argued that the structure of the book can be best understood by seeing it as a unity.

Regarding v. 15, there is wide agreement that the two parts of this text are now in the wrong order. The second half of the verse links with what has preceded, both in form and in content. In particular, it should be noted that the Hebrew underlying the "you"/"your" of the latter part of v. 15 (from "as you have done") is singular; thus it is best understood in the same sense as in the preceding verses, as a reference to Edom. As to content, v. 15a introduces the theme of the punishment of nations, which is to be elaborated in the remainder of the book, whereas v. 15b is an application of the *lex talionis* against Edom (that is to say, punishment corresponding to the offense would be exacted). Edom's offenses have been listed, and it is now asserted that Edom will be the victim of the same punishment which it has taken such pleasure in meting out to others. Often, when a displacement of the existing order of a text is proposed, it is important to look for some motive which has brought about the rearrangement, but here it may be purely accidental. The openings of vv. 15a, 15b, and 16a are all extremely similar in the Hebrew text; all have the same initial letter, and it is likely that at some point a copyist's error has led to their being transmitted in the wrong order.

Verse 15b introduces the theme of just and exact retribution which characterizes a number of passages directed against unjust oppressors of God's people. The theme is found in Ezek. 35:15, where in similar phraseology it is also directed against Edom. The Hebrew word *gemul,* here translated "deeds," provides another link with Ps. 137; there, at v. 8, it occurs in the phrase "with what you have done to us." This particular concept of precise retributive justice is an important element in the foreign nations oracles, and here it makes a natural conclusion to Obad. 11-14. Modern comment on material of this kind often emphasizes the harshness of such a view; at least as important is the need to recognize that retributive justice of this kind also implies that the punishment to be imposed will not *exceed* the fault incurred. "As you have done, it shall be done to you" — that, and no more severe punishment, is implied.

Verse 15a is best understood as the introduction to the remaining verses of the book. Here we find an extension of the theme of divine judgment from one specific enemy nation, Edom, to "all the nations." As we have seen, it is possible that this section comes from a different author, but recent study of this and other prophetic collections has tended to lay the emphasis upon the literary characteristics of a book as a whole rather than upon historical criteria for division into sources. On that account, there is a clear literary link with what precedes, in particular by the continuing use of the word "day." But whereas in the earlier section the "day" was one in which punishment had been wrought upon Judah, here, as in many prophetic oracles, we have the theme of a "day of the LORD" against his enemies.

The prophetic books all regard such a day as one in which the LORD will punish his enemies, but there are two different emphases to be discerned in the identification of those enemies. In some passages, such as Amos 5:18ff.; Zeph. 1:7ff., the enemies are the false worshipers within Yahweh's community. Elsewhere, the day is envisaged as an occasion when all enemies, and in particular foreign nations hostile to the LORD's people, will be consumed. Obadiah is clearly of this latter type, and the emphasis can be paralleled in Isa. 2:12-22 and more closely in 13:6-8 and Jer. 46:10. More striking, however, is the link with Joel 3:2, which speaks of God gathering "all the nations" for judgment. From this point on we shall see numerous similarities between our text and the final chapter of Joel, where the theme of God's judgment is also prominent.

16 Judgment is first expressed through the imagery of drunkenness. The present form of the Hebrew text of Nah. 1:10 uses the same image, but as we saw in our discussion of that passage (above, p. 28), the Hebrew is very obscure and emendation is usual. Here, however, no such doubt arises; the Hebrew verb *shatah* ("to drink") is used three times in the verse. It seems likely that two different images have here been blended together. There is first the idea of the drunkenness associated with victory; the army after its victory would expect rich spoil, including food and drink from the defeated enemy. But their carousing would quickly be turned into drunkenness of another kind: that associated with the "cup of wrath" which the LORD would press upon his enemies (Ps. 75:8).

Once again there are striking parallels within the other collections of prophetic oracles against foreign nations, notably Jer. 49:12, which is a prose insertion into the oracle against Edom. But the same motif is found in fuller form at 25:15-29, and is very characteristic of chs. 46–51. An interesting contrast to our present verse is found in Deutero-Isaiah, which may come from a similar period. At Isa. 51:17-23 part of the promise to Zion is that "the bowl of my wrath you shall drink no more" (v. 22). Obadiah 16, by contrast, makes it clear that there was to be no such remission for other nations: "all the nations round about shall drink . . . and stagger." (As noted in the RSV margin, the translation "stagger" is dependent upon an emendation of an uncertain Hebrew verb; it is possible that the text can be retained, and the verb *l-'-'* be understood as "drink noisily" or the like; so Koehler-Baumgartner.) However this may be, the sense is clear enough, and so is the dramatic end result of this judgment by means of the cup of wrath: "[they] shall be as though they had not been." The utter destruction of those who are the victims of Yahweh's just judgment is proclaimed.

17 It is very clear that a sharp contrast ("But") is introduced in this verse. It is less clear whether this contrast is intended by the prophet as a deliberate means of highlighting the difference from what has preceded or whether it is a later redactional development, emphasizing the status of the chosen community. If the latter view is taken, v. 21 would provide a similar development. But it is perhaps more satisfactory to take vv. 16 and 17 together as setting out the contrasting fates of "all the nations" and "those that escape." The latter phrase can have as its primary thrust the sense of a narrow escape, with the main emphasis on the greatness of the calamity; that sense seems to be present in v. 14, where the word translated "fugitives" is cognate with that here rendered "those that escape." But there also seems to be a sense of those who were delivered from danger as themselves being thereby in a special relation to God, and from this the whole idea of a "remnant theology" emerges.

It is not always easy to distinguish between these two ideas in the prophetic literature, but the remnant theme is particularly prominent in Isaiah. For example, the name given to Isaiah's son, Shear-jashub (Isa. 7:3), means "A remnant shall return." Two particular passages are very close to the idea expressed here in Obadiah: Isa. 4:2 and 10:20, where in each case the cognate word is translated "survivors." This link with Isaiah is also furthered by the strongly Jerusalemite associations found in each case. Despite the destruction of Jerusalem, the divine favor has not been totally removed from the "holy" city.

This theme of Jerusalem as the "holy city" is one that has been of great significance in the thought of Judaism, Christianity, and Islam. Furthermore, it has been of tremendous importance in the political and religious history of the Middle East and, indeed, of much of the rest of the world. Within the Judeo-Christian tradition in particular, this idea of a holy place — be it the whole city or a particular building — is a distinctly ambiguous one. Alongside the reverence for Jerusalem found here and, for example, in Haggai and the work of the Chronicler, there is also a strong note of warning against false trust in any kind of holy place (Jer. 7; Ezek. 16) — a note which can clearly be heard in the NT in, for example, Stephen's speech in Acts 7 (cf. 6:13-14). It is a continuing tension for the community of faith in many places today.

As to the idea of the "holy" city, it is vital to recognize that here, as elsewhere in the OT, the idea of holiness is not simply — or even primarily — a moral and ethical idea. Allen rightly refers

(*Joel, etc.,* 164-65) to a passage in Isaiah which may be approximately contemporary with our prophet. To call Jerusalem "the holy city" implies that

> there shall no more come into you the uncircumcised and the unclean. (Isa. 52:1)

Holiness, that is to say, implies a state of being set apart, and the exclusion of all that is regarded as being incompatible with that state. Both the positive and the potentially negative and damaging aspects of the idea are plain to see.

The second half of the verse may refer to the prospect of dispossessed exiles regaining their lost territory and all that went with it; this is rendered still more likely if, with BHS and most commentators, a slight emendation of the text be accepted so as to read *morishehem* for *morashehem.* This reading, long suggested by the ancient versions, is now supported by the Hebrew scroll of the Minor Prophets found at Murabba'at near the Dead Sea, and would give a rendering such as that found in NEB: "and Jacob shall dispossess those that dispossessed them." There may be a link with the reference in v. 10 to the hostility between Jacob and Edom/Esau, but it is also possible that the point here is a more general one. The designation of Israel as "the house of Jacob" is most frequently found in the Isaiah tradition, and it seems likely that here the reference is to the way in which the Jerusalem community, or at least its leaders, had been sent into exile. A close comparison can be drawn with Isa. 48:1-2, which also speaks of the "house of Jacob" as those whose destiny is inextricably tied to that of the "holy city."

18 A link with what has preceded is supplied by the expression "house of Jacob." However, here it appears that the point of reference is narrower and more specific, that is, the deliberate contrast between Israel and Edom and the fate which is anticipated for each community. Two points of particular concern arise from this verse: first, the particular significance of the imagery of burning; second, the use of remnant language.

"Fire" and its rare synonym here translated "flame" are common OT metaphors of divine judgment. God himself is often pictured as appearing to his worshipers in the fire of theophany (cf. in particular the vivid description of the theophany at Sinai in Exod. 19), and the consequence of this is judgment. But whereas the remarkable feature of the preexilic prophets was that they characteristically envisaged this judgment as coming upon Israel itself (e.g., Amos 3:2), here and in many other later prophetic passages the fire of judgment is something that will destroy Israel's enemies. On the other hand, Israel itself is pictured as the avenging fire by which God's judgment is brought upon his enemies, who are now regarded as identifiable with Israel's own enemies. In this presentation "Jacob" and "Joseph" are treated as synonymous. This would seem strange if we have in mind only the Genesis story, for there Joseph is pictured as Jacob's son. In fact, this synonymous usage occurs sufficiently often elsewhere (e.g., Ps. 77:15) to suggest that it was a standard poetic description.

A transformation of earlier prophetic usage can also be detected in the use of remnant language. It is likely that in those passages from the 8th-cent. prophets which can confidently be regarded as original to the prophets themselves the remnant theme is essentially a threat: "only a remnant" (Isa. 10:22) or, using the same term as is found here, "a few survivors" (Isa. 1:9). It seems, however, as if the emphasis changed, from the threat implicit in the fewness of those who escape, to the promise implicit in the fact that there should be any survivors at all. (On this view the Isaiah passages mentioned in the discussion of v. 17, Isa. 4:2 and 10:20, would be later additions to the original message of Isaiah.) In our present verse the threat and promise elements are both found. The "survivors" of Judah (Obad. 14) will become the instruments of God's action; but for Edom there will be complete destruction. The certainty of such a fate is underlined by the use of the messenger formula, "for the LORD has spoken." Destruction is to be complete, and the very finality of it is set out in a way which anticipates the later apocalyptic writings.

19-20 It is widely agreed among commentators that these two verses reflect a later elaboration of the basic threat. They are set out in the RSV in the form of poetry, and they undoubtedly possess a certain rhythmic character; but they can hardly be regarded as poetry of the type normally found in prophetic oracles, and in critical editions of the text (e.g., BHS) they are set out as prose. Textual uncertainties, some of which will be discussed below, add to the difficulties with regard to the form of these verses.

Some help may, however, be gained by noting one basic feature of this section. Both the listing of different groups and the repeated use of the verb *yarash* ("to possess"), three times in the two verses, remind us of the apportionment of the land to the people when they first possessed it under Joshua. Here, as in the earlier presentation, the theme is of those for the moment outside the promised land being promised an inheritance within it. It is not at all clear whether the list of places represents a specific contemporary geographic distribution of peoples or is intended to have a symbolic significance; the difficulty in resolving this problem is increased by the syntactical difficulties of this section.

Only the barest outline of the textual difficulties can here be set out, and the larger commentaries must be consulted for more detailed discussion. (Wolff and Allen both set out the problems fully, with reference to other discussions of particular details.) We can say at the outset that nothing approaching a consensus of how the problems should be solved has been reached.

19 "Those of the Negeb shall possess Mount Esau." This translation is reached by making the Hebrew word *hannegeb* mean the inhabitants of that area, the desert south of Judah; but it seems more likely that the subject of the (plural) verb should be "they," referring back to the "house of Jacob," and that "the Negeb" is the object. "They shall possess the Negeb" would then be a picture of the fulfillment of ancient promises; the whole extent of the land, including its most distant southern border, would be restored to the possession of those now in exile under foreign rule. If this is correct, then "Mount Esau" would be a gloss (so BHS) applying the more general promise to the specific context of the book of Obadiah, with its anti-Edomite polemic.

An exactly analogous reconstruction would make best sense of the next line, an original "they shall possess the Shephelah" (that is, the lower slopes west of Judah) being glossed by the addition of "the land of the Philistines." The remainder of the verse, however, is more difficult, and precise reconstruction here is very speculative. The expression *sedeh Ephraim* (RSV "the land of Ephraim") is an unusual one, without close parallel in the OT. The word *sadeh* normally means "field," the cultivated area as opposed to the wilderness. It is noteworthy that as long ago as the Greek translation some difficulty was felt as the Greek rendered the expression "the mountain of Ephraim." Probably both this reading and "the land of Samaria" are expansions of the original, but here it is not possible to see any way in which we might discern any immediate relevance to the circumstances of the book of Obadiah. Most probably this particular promise looks forward to the return of the exiles of the northern kingdom, as will be made more explicit in the next verse. Finally, and in some ways most perplexing of all, the verse ends with the cryptic expression "and Benjamin Gilead." Though both the RSV and the NEB take this as a promise comparable to those which have preceded and accordingly supply the verb "shall possess," it is perhaps more likely that one of these nouns is a later elaboration.

In the end, therefore, the understanding of the verse which has most to commend it may be one which sees the "house of Jacob" as being given the promise of possessing the Negeb, the Shephelah, Ephraim, and Gilead; moreover, this promise would have been elaborated by a later glossator with an explanatory comment upon each name in accordance with the circumstances of his own day. If something along these lines should be correct, the verse can be understood both as a reflection upon the original giving of the land by Yahweh to his people, and as a promise to his contemporary worshipers.

20 Textual difficulties remain acute in this verse. The problem in making sense of the first half as it stands can be seen from a literal rendering such as that of the RV (the italicized words are additions to give meaning to the text): "And the captivity of this host of the children of Israel which are *among* the Canaanites *shall possess* even unto Zarephath." Fortunately, however, the general sense can probably be recovered, even when precise reconstruction of the text cannot be established with certainty. As in the previous verse, the picture is one of the restoration of the exiled people. If the emendation followed by the RSV be accepted, that of reading *bahalah* ("in Halah") for *hahel-hazzeh* ("this host"), then the reference would be specifically to the exiled inhabitants of the former northern kingdom for whom Halah, near Nineveh, had been one of the places to which they had been deported (2 Kgs. 17:6).

The next difficulty comes in the Hebrew phrase that can be

literally translated "who are Canaanites." This scarcely makes
sense as it stands, and modern versions almost without exception
emend it. The RV, as noted above, inserts "among the" in order
to obtain acceptable sense. The RSV treats "Canaanites" as
equivalent to "Phoenicia" and emends the relative word *asher* to
some form of the verb *yarash* ("to possess"), which has already
occurred three times in v. 19 and the latter part of this verse. As
is so often the case, it is easier to engage in a reconstruction of
this kind which makes good sense than to explain why so natural
a rendering should ever have been lost. It is therefore unlikely
that we can claim a precise reconstruction of a lost original.
Nevertheless, the underlying point seems to be a promise that
those once in exile would possess the land of the Canaanites as
far as Zarephath. This settlement near Sidon is mentioned both
at 1 Kgs. 17:9 and at Luke 4:26 as symbolizing a Gentile area,
in the former case as a city outside the borders of Israel, in the
latter as a typical heathen city. Here the point would be, first,
that even such alien territory would come within Israel's control
and, second, that the southern extension referred to in vv. 19 and
20 will be matched by new northern possessions.

In the remainder of the verse no textual emendation seems to
be called for, and the theme of returned exiles being given an
extension of territory is the same as that of the first part of the
verse. (Indeed, the statement of the theme here gives more confidence in such an interpretation in the preceding part of the
verse.) The difficulty here relates to the expression "who are in
Sepharad," an unknown location, and one which is sometimes
deleted as a gloss (cf. BHS). Sardis in Asia Minor, islands off the
African coast, a site in Media, and (the traditional interpretation)
Spain all have been proposed, but we must confess to continuing
ignorance. The name is not found elsewhere in the OT, unless,
following Michael C. Astour (*IDBS*, 807), we identify Sepharad
with Sepharvaim, another of the places to which the exiles of the
northern kingdom were taken (cf. by implication 2 Kgs. 17:24).
It is an attractive suggestion, but the emendation has no external
support, and it suffers from the obvious weakness that Sepharvaim is linked only with the exile of the northerners, whereas the
reference here is to "the exiles of Jerusalem." In view of our
ignorance of much historical detail, it is probably wise to acknowledge that we cannot locate Sepharad with any certainty.

In any case, the reference to "the Negeb" at the end of the verse represents an inclusio demarking vv. 19-20 as a distinct unit begun and ended with a reference to the Negeb, the desert area to the south of the promised land which would, in the promises of God, come to be incorporated within that land.

21 This final verse is reminiscent of v. 17. It is an ending closely comparable to the "hopeful" addition to the end of Amos, which likewise envisaged salvation for Israel in terms of possessing "the remnant of Edom" (Amos 9:12); Isa. 11:14, also an elaboration of the original prophetic words, expresses closely similar ideas. Theologically, three points are being made which must be held together for their proper understanding. First, there is the conviction that "saviors" will be raised up. The plural form is unusual (though cf. Neh. 9:27), but it is better to keep the Hebrew text than to emend to a passive form, as proposed by BHS: "those who are saved." These "saviors" will once more reactivate the traditions associated with "Mount Zion" and proclaim victory there. Second, that victory will be over all who oppose God's will, symbolized here as in most of Obadiah by "Mount Esau." The reference is once again not a simple matter of geography, but evokes rivalry between mountains as comparable to claims for different gods. Third, all this will be an effective means of displaying the rule of Yahweh himself. The phrase "the kingdom shall be the LORD's" is virtually identical with Ps. 22:28 (RSV "dominion belongs to the LORD") and closely reminiscent of many other phrases in the Psalms. This suggests that we have here a link with the Jerusalem cult, in which the kingship of Yahweh appears to have been a prominent theme. The promises made in that cult had not been illusory; the divine rule could still properly be upheld and proclaimed.

This provides a characteristic note on which to leave the words of Obadiah. To the end there is maintained the tension between the general assertion of Yahweh's power, with the conviction that he would overthrow all his enemies, and the specific application of that power to the struggle against the Edomites, who for the author of this short collection epitomized the work of those enemies.

BIBLIOGRAPHY

Commentaries

Allen, L. C. *The Books of Joel, Obadiah, Jonah and Micah*. New International Commentary on the Old Testament (Grand Rapids: Wm. B. Eerdmans and London: Hodder and Stoughton, 1976).

Rudolph, W. *Joel – Amos – Obadja – Jona*. Kommentar zum Alten Testament (Gütersloh: Gerd Mohn, 1971).

Smith, J. M. P., W. H. Ward, and J. A. Bewer. *Micah, Zephaniah, Nahum, Habakkuk, Obadiah and Joel*. International Critical Commentary (Edinburgh: T. & T. Clark and New York: Scribners, 1911).

Watts, J. D. W. *The Books of Joel, Obadiah, Jonah, Nahum, Habakkuk and Zephaniah*. Cambridge Bible Commentary (Cambridge and New York: Cambridge University Press, 1975).

————. *Obadiah: A Critical Exegetical Commentary* (Grand Rapids: Wm. B. Eerdmans, 1969).

Wolff, H. W. *Dodekapropheten 3: Obadja und Jona*. Biblischer Kommentar: Altes Testament (Neukirchen-Vluyn: Neukirchener Verlag, 1977).

Other Works Cited

Astour, M. C. "Sepharad," *Interpreter's Dictionary of the Bible*, Supplement, ed. K. R. Crim (Nashville: Abingdon, 1976), 807.

Bartlett, J. R. "The Brotherhood of Edom," *Journal for the Study of the Old Testament* 4 (1977): 2-27.

————. "The Moabites and Edomites," in *Peoples of OT Times*, ed. D. J. Wiseman (Oxford and New York: Oxford University Press, 1973), 229-58.

Clark, D. J., and N. Mundhenk. *A Translator's Handbook on the Books of Obadiah and Micah* (London and New York: United Bible Societies, 1982).

Eissfeldt, O. *The OT: An Introduction* (Oxford: Blackwell and New York: Harper & Row, 1965).

Jerrome, P. "The Book of Obadiah," in *Readings in Biblical Hebrew* 2, ed. J. H. Eaton (Birmingham: University of Birmingham, 1978).

Pfeiffer, R. H. *Introduction to the OT*, rev. ed. (New York and London: Harper, 1948).

Soggin, J. A. *Introduction to the OT*, trans. J. Bowden. Old Testament Library (Philadelphia: Westminster and London: SCM, 1976).

EPILOGUE TO
NAHUM AND OBADIAH

In the modern Western world tolerance is regarded, broadly speaking, as a desirable characteristic. In matters of religion and politics it is often urged upon children from a young age that they must try to respect and understand the views of those who differ from them, to tolerate diversity, and, indeed, even to welcome and encourage it.

Yet alongside this attitude there is ample evidence that in many contexts such a viewpoint not only is not shared, but is even regarded as a betrayal. Fundamentalist religious leaders, whether they be Muslims in Iran or Christians in many Western countries, do not regard other faiths as something to be tolerated and learned about, but as the work of evil powers. It is this latter attitude that has been characteristic of much of the religious history of our world rather than the easy tolerance of some parts of the modern West (where, too, it is not difficult to see that such tolerance is only acceptable within certain clearly defined limits).

Reflections such as these are relevant when studying prophetic books such as Nahum and Obadiah, which only express in a more direct and vivid form what is implicit in large parts of the Bible, NT as well as OT. Throughout the Bible life is presented as a struggle between a clear right and an equally clear wrong, and the wrong is not always spiritualized in the kind of way which we nowadays might find less embarrassing. What Nahum anticipates for Nineveh and Obadiah for Edom is a fate which, according to the Gospel of Matthew, Jesus envisages for the scribes and Pharisees of his day, whom he calls "children of hell" (Matt. 23:15). Issues of this kind should be sharply focused by our study of these two prophetic books.

To make assertions of this kind is not to imply that we simply accept the viewpoint of the biblical writers and then try to square it as best we can with our own convictions and consciences. There is more than one sense in which the Bible comes to us from a remote world. Not only have Assyria and Edom disappeared from the atlas; much of what Nahum and Obadiah thought about God and his dealings with humanity has also disappeared from our consciousness. Yet there is another sense in which these strange books express a truth that is at the very heart of a theistic perception of the world. They proclaim that our world is an ordered world, that God is in control, that all which appears hostile to his purposes will undergo judgment. We do not have to imitate those prophets, or express our beliefs in the way that they did. We nevertheless do well to acknowledge their lasting insights into the nature of humanity and its ambiguous relationship to God.

THE
FAITHFULNESS
OF GOD

A Commentary on the Book of
Esther

S. PAUL RE'EMI

CONTENTS

INTRODUCTION

The book of Esther presents us at the outset with three problems:
historical, literary, and cultic.

1. THE HISTORICAL PROBLEM

The writer probably intended to write history. He set out to
describe a historical event that happened in his time or shortly
before, an event which, he believed, ought to be remembered by
later generations. Some scholars, however, question the authen-
ticity of various aspects of the book. The name Ahasuerus is a
good Persian one, and it may be translated Xerxes, though in
the LXX it is rendered Artaxerxes. The wife of the historical
Xerxes bore the name, not Vashti or Esther, but Hutaossa (in
Greek Atossa). At the time of this story Xerxes was busy with
his Greek war or at least with preparations for it, and was unlikely to have had time for banqueting in his palace at Susa.
Mordecai, who went into captivity with King Jeconiah (Esth.
2:6) in the period of the book of Esther, would be by now at least
120 years old. We may add even more inner improbabilities; for
example, we cannot imagine that a king of Persia would permit
his own subjects to be slaughtered by a foreign people.

Other scholars believe that the book is built on a mythological
basis derived from a poem concerning the battle between the
Babylonian deities Marduk and Ishtar, on the one hand, and the
Elamite gods Humman and Vashti, on the other. Yet we know
from history that the wife of the Elamite god was not Vashti but
Kiri-rishna, i.e., Seres (Heb. *Zeresh;* Esth. 6:13). The similarity
of the name is remarkable and cannot be just accidental. Until
now, however, no one has succeeded in finding an appropriate
myth to link the story of Esther with Persian legends dealing with
the Persian New Year.

Increasingly today, however, the suggestion is made that our little book may be understood to be in the nature of a historical novel. Such a story would then be built upon certain known facts available to the writer, and reflect the relations that obtained between the Jews and the Persians and other peoples of the day. And it is possible that a persecution of the Jews, even if limited, did actually take place during the rebellion of the satraps under Artaxerxes II (404-358 B.C.). So we are not to consider this book as being "only a story." It is clear that the author reflects deep knowledge of the political life of the Persian Empire as well as its social customs.

Although Ahasuerus could not be Xerxes I, he could be Artaxerxes II, also called Mnemon. He was appointed king at the death of his father Darius II, since he was his firstborn son. But such a nomination was against Persian law. According to it the successor had to be the firstborn, but he also had to be nominated while his parents were still on the throne. On the basis of this law the king's younger brother Cyrus claimed his rights to the throne, and then conspired against his older brother. Cyrus's conspiracy was discovered by Hapartes Tissaphernes, a member of the royal court. Cyrus was caught and condemned to death, only the tears of his mother saving his life. He was exiled, but continued to conspire, and soon gathered an army with the help of the Spartans. Cyrus met his brother Artaxerxes at the battle of Cunaxa, where he was defeated and lost his life.

These events took place 2½ years after Artaxerxes gained the throne, and only then did he feel safe enough to celebrate his coronation. He ordered a sumptuous banquet for his commanders and nobles three years after his accession (cf. Esth. 1:2-3). These leaders the king invited to his banquet, while the queen held her own banquet separately with the ladies. The queen's name was Amestris. It is possible, however, that she received the name "Vashti," which in Persian means "beautiful." She was the daughter of a Parthian leader called Hidranes. For some unknown reason the queen mother hated Hidranes and gave orders to have him killed along with his household. She also hated Queen Amestris, who robbed her of her influence at the court, and waited for an opportunity to get rid of her. This opportunity came when Artaxerxes, full of liquor, ordered the queen to display her beauty to the nobles at the banquet. The queen refused to do so, as it was against the reigning customs of the modesty of women. This refusal kindled the anger of the king, who, according to ancient sources, was weak and vain. He called upon the nobles of the Privy Council to pass judgment upon her. They condemned the queen to be dethroned, as the best way out of this delicate situation. But the queen mother used this opportunity of Amestris's disgrace to poison her.

In order to console the king in his sorrow, the nobles advised him to find a successor for the late queen. Thus messengers were dispatched throughout the empire to gather in beautiful virgins from among whom the king might choose a spouse. It is possible then that this is the context in which we are to understand the story of Esther. Then in regard to Mordecai, we assume that it was not actually Mordecai but one of his ancestors, probably Kish the Benjamite, who was among the Judean exiles who left Jerusalem with King Jeconiah in 596. Mordecai is a Persian name (from the god Marduk) and so is not likely to have been given to a child born in Judah. The name of his adopted daughter, Esther, is also of Persian origin (from the goddess Ishtar); her Hebrew name Hadassah means "myrtle," but it too could have originated in the Persian name Atossa.

Therefore, we would suggest that the book of Esther was written by a person who knew about such events, but who saw them as an example of God's saving providence for his people Israel. The event was remembered and relived by the whole Jewish community in later years in the annual celebration of the Feast of Purim. This then was "history" that shaped their lives.

It is true that a scholar like Joshua ben Sira (Jesus the son of Sirach), in his chapters on "the fathers of the world" (Sir. 44 – 50), mentions neither Mordecai nor Esther. On the other hand, he also omits all reference to Ezra the scribe, recognized by all Jews as the great spiritual leader of his nation. Besides, there is no doubt that the book of Esther was completed in a period later than Ben Sira, who lived about 200 B.C. It was possibly compiled from documents left by the Jews of Susa, or even by Esther and Mordecai themselves. This story of Mordecai and Esther then reached Judah at a later date. The First Book of Maccabees does not mention the Feast of Purim, as it was celebrated largely in the Diaspora. But in 2 Maccabees, composed about one hundred years later, we read how the people celebrated the day of Nicanor

107

one day before the "day of Mordecai" (2 Macc. 15:36). Some historians, like Cecil Roth, take the history of Esther seriously. Roth writes: "We are informed of a persecution throughout the Persian Empire which was foiled through the influence at court of a Jewish woman, named Esther" (*A Short History of the Jewish People*, 64). Such persecutions undoubtedly took place during the reign of Artaxerxes II, the reason for them lying not so much in any personal enmity between Haman and Mordecai as in the contradiction between the religion of the Jews and that of the Persians. In the time of Artaxerxes II important reforms were introduced into the religion of Zoroaster, which had been in its beginnings a belief in an abstract God. But Artaxerxes introduced deities from other nations as well and required all his subjects to worship them. This provoked the opposition of the orthodox Persians as well as the orthodox Jews. In consequence, there followed persecutions against those who opposed the new cult. Mordecai, who was not an orthodox Jew, nevertheless took up the defense of his brethren and succeeded therein with the help of his adopted daughter Esther, who was then the spouse of the king of Persia.

2. THE LITERARY PROBLEM

The literary composition of the book of Esther shows quite a complicated relationship. The book has reached us in at least three forms. One is in Hebrew and two are in Greek. In a later period (8th cent. A.D.) there were also added two Targums (translations into Aramaic containing a certain amount of exposition), mostly from haggadic and talmudic sources. Concerning the Greek translations, we have the LXX with or without Additions, and the Lucianic Text, which is shorter and rather different from the LXX. Most commentators accept the Hebrew version as the original one and so the older, regarding the Greek versions as a later development. These seek to give a more religious character to the book, for in Hebrew the impression made is largely secular.

From the literary point of view the book of Esther is a unity, except for the double account of the administration of Purim in ch. 9. The book seems, however, to follow traditions and motifs from different sources. The story of the feast at the beginning can be considered as an independent story. Two different motifs can then be distinguished in the book, that of Esther and that of Mordecai and Haman. Yet both motifs are so fused that it is not easy to separate them in a mechanical way. It is significant that in the first announcement about the celebration of the feast, when Mordecai proclaims the royal order, he does not mention Esther as a reason for the feast (9:20-22); moreover, when the Feast of Purim is mentioned in the oldest sources, it is called the day of Mordecai. The question thus arises, are there then here really two traditions?

Concerning the Esther motif, it can be said that much of its content is connected with various legends and stories that go back to the Persian New Year. The same can be said about the story of the banquet. This material would then be available to the Jewish author of this "book of Esther."

According to other commentators the author drew his material from a midrashic source containing stories of various Jewish heroes and heroines as well as of persecutions. They presume that the author combined into one work three separate and unrelated stories: (1) the Vashti story, which could have been originally an apocryphal "harem" story; (2) the story of Mordecai, which is concerned with court intrigue, jealousy, and persecutions in Susa; and (3) the story of Esther, which told about a young Jewess who, after becoming the favorite of the king, intervened to prevent certain persecutions of her people. That ethical problems are overlooked when the safety of the Jewish people is at stake is understandable, since we have a similar tale in the story of Rahab (Josh. 2:1; 6:17, 25). Carey A. Moore compares the story of Esther to a lustrous pearl, which "consists of a hard core of sand around which successive layers of colorful foreign substance have accumulated" (*Esther*, LIII). The book of Esther has certainly a historical core, the story of Mordecai and perhaps that of Esther, to which have been added legendary and pictorial elements, notably the story of Vashti and the banquet of the king.

3. DATE AND PLACE OF COMPOSITION

One thing is certain—neither Mordecai nor Esther wrote the book. Mordecai could not write: "In those days when king Ahasuerus sat on his royal throne" (Esth. 1:2). The style fits a story about an event in the past. The writer speaks about Purim as a fixed feast (9:19) that has been accepted by the people for a long time. Mordecai was a part of the history of the Persian Empire (10:2). Some commentators suppose that the book was written in the time of the Maccabees (2nd cent. B.C.) on the basis of the notes of Mordecai and Esther, as well as of others who were then at the king's court and knew its customs well. These historical notes were written, they maintain, into "the book of Esther" (9:20, 29).

Popular imagination then may have added to the historical report or perhaps exaggerated its details, as for example the number of those killed (9:16). The Feast of Purim is really a feast marking the spirit of deliverance from one's enemies. The decree of Haman was restricted to the central provinces; that is why it was known in Judah only much later. This may be the reason why it was not mentioned in 1 Maccabees. It was written about a hundred years later (2 Macc. 15:35-36).

It is significant that more Persian words occur in the book of Esther than in any other biblical book composed in the Persian period, such as Haggai, Zechariah, Malachi, Ezra, and Nehemiah. The last two personalities had actually resided near or in the royal court. In the book of Esther there occur sixty Persian words in 167 verses, while in Ezra and Nehemiah there are only fifty-five in 700 verses. This means that Esther was written primarily for Jews who spoke Persian. Some conclude therefore that the scroll was written in Persia and not in Israel. The feast, they suggest, was probably celebrated first in Central Persia. That is why Queen Esther had to write a second letter to enforce the holding of the feast (9:29).

In fixing the date of Esther's composition we must distinguish between the first and the final versions. Our Hebrew text is closest to the completed text which the rabbis approved, and from which our present Masoretic Text probably descends.

4. THE CULTIC PROBLEM

Concerning the origins of the Feast of Purim, there are a number of hypotheses, but no general agreement. Four facts are clear. (1) The word *pur* is not a Hebrew word, nor is it Persian; it is Akkadian, meaning "a lot" or "destiny." (2) The casting of lots does not play, in this story, a role sufficient to explain the meaning of the feast. It is possible that casting lots was a custom among the Babylonian Jews, thus giving a popular etymological explanation of the Persian name. (3) The Purim feast contains some features connected with the New Year celebrations in Persia, such as, for instance, the presenting of gifts, sham gifts, and the casting of lots. (4) Herodotus informs us of a Persian feast called "Magophonia" (i.e., "the killing of Magi") which was celebrated in memory of Smerdes, a usurper under Darius I. This report may have suggested a reason for the feast in the book of Esther.

It is also possible that the Jews in Persia or in Babylonia had accepted certain customs connected with the Persian New Year. A Persian name, though of Akkadian origin, could thus have been taken over from some legendary material of old. We cannot prove that there was some connection between the persecutions of the Jews and the celebration of the Persian New Year, but it is not impossible. Such feasts could excite religious fanaticism and incite their participants to attack the "infidels," that is, those who held a different faith.

The religious significance of the feast is, perhaps, not great. The Hebrew version avoids even the use of the name of God. Yet it should be stressed that the author considered its happenings as guided by the providence of God. Mordecai waited for help from God only in case Esther should refuse her help (4:14). Thus the name "Jew" is used here more in an ethnic sense than in a religious one (8:17). The principal feature of the book is national rather than religious, though the two conceptions were for the author inseparable.

The tractate *Megillah* (the Hebrew name for "scroll") in the Mishnah deals with the cultic side of the Feast of Purim. This account is composed of different strata; Rabbi Meir's collection of material is based on that of his teacher, Rabbi Akiba (ca. A.D. 135). It states that "if the Megillah has been read in the first Adar and the year has subsequently been prolonged [by the intercalation of a second Adar; the Jews used the lunar year, and so at intervals had to correct it with their solar year], it is read again in the second Adar" (*Megillah* 6b).

Between the periods when the Feast of Purim was celebrated in Persia, following the decrees of Mordecai and Esther, and its acceptance by rabbinic sources there is a wide gap. Yet an anonymous Baraitha ("comment") on the Talmud shows that Purim was already celebrated in the last decades of the temple; for it prescribes that the priests should interrupt their service in the temple, and the Levites their singing, and the representatives of the people their attendance at public sacrifices, in order to go and listen to the reading of the *Megillah*.

5. CANONICITY

There is no reason to doubt that the book of Esther was recognized as canonical at the Council of Jamnia (A.D. 90), as one of the twenty-four books of the Jewish canon of the OT (*Baraitha* in *Baba Bathra* 14b-15a of the Babylonian Talmud, 2nd cent. A.D.). The grounds for its canonicity at Jamnia were: (1) the book gives an exact account of events, describing how the Jewish community in Persia was saved from complete extinction; and (2) it provided a reason for a popular religious festival full of joy in the days of sorrow after the destruction of the temple in A.D. 70. The Jewish community could thus find in it consolation and hope that another Mordecai or Esther would rise up to save the people from their distress.

Among the Christians of the West the book of Esther was almost always accepted as canonical, while in the East very often it was not the case. Bishop Athanasius denied Esther's canonical status, yet included the book — together with Judith and Tobit — as being edifying for the Church because the courage of Judith is likened to that of Esther. The book of Esther was finally received into the Christian canon at the Council of Carthage in A.D. 397.

6. GREEK VERSION

Besides the Hebrew text the only other witness to the original text is the Greek translation, the LXX. Esther is the only book of the Greek OT, except The Wisdom of Jesus the Son of Sirach, that has a superscription containing information about its authorship and date. According to the Addition F, v. 11:

> In the fourth of the reign of Ptolemy and Cleopatra, Dositheus, who said that he was a priest and a Levite, and

Ptolemy his son brought to Egypt the preceding Letter of Purim, which they said was genuine and had been translated by Lysimachus the son of Ptolemy, one of the residents of Jerusalem.

This means that this Greek translation was brought from Jerusalem to Egypt in the fourth year of the reign of a king named Ptolemy who was married to Cleopatra. The only king whose consort was Cleopatra in the fourth year of his reign was Ptolemy VIII (117-108 B.C.). Thus the book may be assigned to the year 114 B.C.

The Greek text differs from the Hebrew in four important ways: (1) it contains a number of additions; (2) it exhibits many omissions; (3) it reveals some basic inconsistencies with the MT; and (4) it explicitly states a religious concern. Some commentators believe that the Additions expound the points of view of their authors and were probably added at a later date. But this does not preclude their being very much alive in the oral tradition of the people.

The manuscript of Codex B (Vaticanus) dates from the 4th century. The A Text, or the Lucianic Text, is an independent translation of the Hebrew text and is considerably shorter than the LXX (B Text). It was prepared by Lucian, martyr of Nicomedia, about A.D. 311.

7. PURPOSE

The book of Esther has always been a favorite of the Jewish people. It has brought them comfort and consolation in difficult times, whether in the period of the Maccabees, in the Middle Ages, or in modern times when persecution reached its terrible climax in the Holocaust in Europe. For it reminds them, as it does the Christian, that God is both faithful and powerful to save, and will never let his people go.

It is possible that the reader could be shocked by the number of enemies slain by the Jews in self-defense (ch. 9). However, we should consider that the numbers were supplied by a chronicler at a later period who undoubtedly felt himself free to exaggerate. Nevertheless, the writer wished to show that God is mighty to help even in the most desperate of situations. What he wants to say is that no human power can finally obstruct God's plan and purpose of salvation, nor thwart God's loyalty to his Covenant; for by means of it he had chosen to use his own people for the redemption of all mankind. God is able to rescue the helpless and the weak from the hands of their cruel oppressors; yet though merciful and gracious, he is also terrible in judgment against those who oppose his purpose of love for the world. God had once called upon the pagan Persian monarch Cyrus to release his chosen people from bondage in Babylonia (Isa. 45:1). Surely then he would always be able to raise up a new Moses when he was needed, for here he had raised up this time a woman, Esther, a "Star," to reveal that his mighty acts of redemptive love never cease.

CHAPTER 1

AHASUERUS'S BANQUET AND THE DISGRACE OF VASHTI
Esther 1:1-22

The Greek version precedes the MT narrative with a kind of prologue, in which Mordecai has a dream in the second year of King Artaxerxes. This employs the typical apocalyptic imagery of the intertestamental period and reminds us of parts of Ezekiel and Daniel. Mordecai sees in his dream a day of gloom and darkness that visits the earth. The entire nation, facing death, cries out to God. Then suddenly there arises as from a tiny spring a mighty river which brings salvation to the people of Israel. This tiny spring is Esther, whom the king has married and made his queen. Esther was thus an instrument in God's hand to save his people.

As Mordecai was dozing in the king's court, he overheard two of the king's eunuchs conspiring to kill the king. Mordecai informed the king about the danger; the two eunuchs were convicted and executed. These two eunuchs were friends of Haman, who enjoyed great favor at the court.

In this chapter in the Hebrew of the OT we have an introductory episode which narrates events that preceded and even led to the elevation of Esther to her high position. This story seems to have its own theme, which has little to do with the main subject. It is possible that the matter comes from a separate source, for it is only at v. 19b that the narrative brings us to Esther.

1-3 "In those days when King Ahasuerus sat on his royal throne . . .," "in the third year of his reign. . . ." Here the author gives us a narrative about a historical character from the past. He tells us also about the vast extent of the empire that stretched from

India to Ethiopia (Nubia), comprising more than 127 provinces, which reminds us of the 127 satrapies mentioned in the book Daniel (Dan. 6:1). Some commentators think that this number is an exaggeration, since from the Greek source only twenty-nine or thirty satrapies are known to us in the Persian Empire.

Moreover, this passage presents some difficulties. If Ahasuerus refers to Xerxes I, then during the first year of his reign this king was occupied with the war against the Greeks (480-470). Being at war with Greece, he would not have had time for banquets. Thus the events of his life do not correspond to the story in the book of Esther.

Others believe that Ahasuerus was rather Artaxerxes II Mnemon (404-358). There could have been political reasons why his name was concealed, though in the LXX he is named Artaxerxes. The LXX also suggests that the cause of this banquet was his marriage (v. 5), while the Lucianic version suggests that it was in order "to celebrate his deliverance." Many centuries ago this thesis was supported by Bar Hebraeus (A.D. 1250).

4-5 The banquet took place with great splendor in Susa, one of the royal residences, and it lasted for 180 days. The description of the palace is confirmed by modern excavations, which prove that the author had a good knowledge of the place. "And when these days were completed" the king gave a banquet lasting seven days for his subjects in the courts of the royal garden. Greek historians, such as Xenophon, confirm that such banquets in the East were held with great luxury and splendor (cf. also Dan. 3:2ff.). It was the custom also to hold them over a long period of days (cf. Jdt. 1:16). These historians tell us that the kings of Persia used to order great feasts especially at New Year and at the festival of Mithrahan, to which they invited their nobles and high officials.

6-8 Although the great riches and luxury exhibited at the palace have a fabulous ring about them, these are confirmed from the Greek writers. "Drinks were served in golden goblets," free for all who wanted them. In the Hebrew the phrase is "without compulsion," noted particularly because it was the Persian custom that everyone had to drink what was put before him.

9 At the same time Queen Vashti "gave a banquet for the

women." The name of the queen, the wife of Artaxerxes, following the Chronicler, was Stateira (an abbreviation from Asta-teira or Vashta-teira), meaning "the beauty of the sign of Mercury." Some say that it comes from the Old Persian *Vahista* ("the best," "the desired," "the beloved"). It was an accepted social custom in those days that decent women should not mix in parties with men, especially when the consumption of wine was so abundant.

10-14   Thus the stage was set. Now the action could begin. "On the seventh day," i.e., on the last day, when the king was full of liquor, he ordered Queen Vashti to come with her royal crown to show off her beauty to the guests. But Vashti refused, possibly because she found it indecent or forbidden by a Persian law of modesty. Some infer that she came from a noble family and so refused to obey the mere whim of a drunken king. But the wrath of the king was kindled and he ordered his Privy Council, composed of seven princes, to judge the stubborn queen.

15-18   One of the princes, Memucan, took the matter very seriously and judged it to be not only an offense against the king but also a bad example for the rest of the empire. So he proposed, and it was decided, that Vashti should be dethroned and should no more appear before the king. Thus there would be set an example throughout the whole empire that wives should respect their husbands. In the verses which follow we learn of the irrevocability of kingly decrees (cf. 3:1-5; 8:8-14).

19-22   The king was pleased with the decision of the Council and gave his royal assent. Letters were sent by special messengers to all the provinces in their respective languages. There were three official languages in the Persian Empire: Old Persian, Babylonian, and Elamite. But this time an exception was made, and the decree was printed or written in the language of each particular nation.

What happened to Vashti? Some suppose that she was exiled from the king's palace. The Midrash (Hebrew homiletic comment) indicates she was condemned to death.

CHAPTER 2

ESTHER CHOSEN QUEEN
Esther 2:1-23

1-2 "After these things. . . ." The author does not specify how long it took the king's anger to abate. But his servants, seeing the king's anger, sought to distract him and advised him to look for another spouse.

3-4 So with the king's assent orders were sent to officers in all provinces to gather "beautiful young virgins" from among whom the king could choose his consort. Some commentators see here a contradiction of an old Persian law, according to which the king had to choose his spouse from seven of the most noble families.

5-7 Here the author interrupts the report on the preparations for the election of the queen in order to introduce the two main characters in the book, Mordecai and Esther. Mordecai was the son of Jair, son of Shimei, son of Kish, a Benjamite who had been taken into captivity with King Jeconiah of Judah. It seems improbable that Mordecai could have been among the exiles of Judah in 597 B.C., for by the time of his nomination as a vizier he would have been at least 127 years old. Thus it seems more probable that it was his ancestor Kish who was carried away into exile, and that Mordecai as well as Esther was born in Babylon (see Introduction). Mordecai's position at the court is not clearly defined (3:3; 8:15); possibly he had some honorary function, e.g., "sitting at the gate" with other dignitaries and officials.

Mordecai had brought up Hadassa (which in Hebrew means "myrtle"). She was the daughter of his uncle Abihail. Now an orphan, she had been left in his care. Her second name, Esther, seems to be of Babylonian origin, from the goddess Ishtar ("a star") or Mercury.

Mordecai's genealogical origin is of no little importance for
the author, who wishes to emphasize that Mordecai was a de-
scendant of Kish, the father of Saul, God's chosen king who had
fought the Amalekites. He would thus be a natural adversary of
Haman, for the latter was descended from Agag the Amalekite
(3:1). It seems that Mordecai belonged to the assimilated nobility
of his adopted country. He had thus no qualms about Esther
being elected to the king's court. The LXX, which always seeks
to explain the events of the OT to the Greek-speaking Jews,
interprets these happenings as directed by the providence of God
for the salvation of his people in this time of distress, just as
Joseph was once sent to be the second to Pharaoh to save his
family from starvation (Gen. 50:20).

8-9 When the king's orders reached the officers of the provinces,
they gathered all likely maidens to Susa, the capital, where they
were under the custody of Hegai. Esther was among them. She
found favor in the eyes of Hegai, who provided her with oint-
ments and food, and sent her also seven maidens to wait on her.
The number seven was especially significant in Persian thought
and customs. For example, the supreme deity had seven superior
beings in attendance; the earthly king had seven princes in his
Privy Council (1:14) and seven eunuchs in attendance upon him.

10-11 Esther in her modesty never forgot her obligation to her
adopted father, and following his advice she did not reveal her
religion or her nationality. This makes us suspect some antago-
nism among the people or at court against the Jews as a people
with a different religion. Following the MT, the author does not
see any fault in the conduct of Esther. He seems of a different
spirit from the authors of Daniel and Ezra. Yet the Additions to
the LXX reveal the deep remorse of Esther at transgressing the
law of her people (see Addition C, vv. 12ff.). Mordecai continued
to care for her; every day he came close to the court of the harem
to inquire about her well-being.

12-14 Those maidens who were to be presented to the king
were beforehand to go through a treatment of beautification lasting about a year. Here again we note that the author is well
acquainted with the customs of the land, for according to ancient

119

sources such was in fact the custom in the kingdoms of the Medes
and Persians.

15-18   Esther followed the good advice of her custodian Hegai,
and did not put on too many ornaments when she went to the
king. In doing so she pleased the king. Perhaps he was attracted
to her because he saw in her an integrity of character arising
from her faith of which the usual pagan Persian women knew
nothing. He fell in love with her, and made her his queen in place
of Vashti (v. 17), four years after he had got rid of the former
queen (v. 16). The king was evidently happy with his new queen
and "gave a great banquet to all his princes and servants" in her
honor. Gifts were distributed, and taxes remitted as a token of
royal liberality.

19-23   In this short passage we learn about the conspiracy of
Bigthan and Teresh, which the LXX introduces at the beginning
of the book. How did Mordecai learn about the intention of those
men to kill the king? This is not explained. The two Aramaic
Targums of Esther, which are not earlier than the 8th cent. A.D.,
give different explanations. One suggests that Mordecai knew
many languages and understood the foreign courtiers, who did
not suspect he could follow them as they talked together. The
other explains that Mordecai learned about it by the Holy Spirit.
Such conspiracies to assassinate a king were not unknown at the
Persian court. After only forty-five days of his reign Xerxes II
was assassinated by his half-brother Secydianus (Sogdianus),
who in turn was killed by Darius II, father of Artaxerxes II Mnemon. It seems that in those days some held the opinion that
human life could be sacrificed on the altar of political ambition,
just as it has been so tragically exhibited in our day. Mordecai
reported the information he had received about the conspiracy
to Queen Esther, who told the king. The affair was investigated,
and the men were found guilty and executed. This deed was
recorded in the royal chronicles to Mordecai's credit.

Why did the king not reward Mordecai for his loyal and cou-
rageous deed? Scholars give different explanations. Some think
that the reward was offered but was lost through inefficient bu-
reaucracy. Others suggest that it was delayed by the providence
of God until the dramatic moment when Haman planned the
destruction of the Jewish people.

CHAPTER 3

HAMAN'S PLOT
Esther 3:1-15

---

1 "After these things . . ." is a common biblical idiom to indicate an indefinite lapse of time or to join loosely together different episodes in a story (e.g., Gen. 15:1). The event related took place twelve years after the king's accession to the throne (Esth. 3:7).

Some commentators suggest that the name Haman takes its origin from Husman, that of an Elamite god who was equal in power and authority to the Persian god Marduk. The attribute "Agagite" denotes his family. The author sought to draw attention to Haman's connection with the people of Amalek, whose King Agag had been the enemy of the people under King Saul (1 Sam. 15:8). This enmity dated from still more ancient times (Num. 24:7). The rabbinical sources connect Haman with Agag, the king of Amalek, as they connect Mordecai with Kish, the father of Saul, showing thereby the traditional enmity between Israel and Amalek that continued for generations (Exod. 17:16). But following the LXX the full name of Haman was "Haman of Amadatus the Bougaian," the name Bougaian originating from the Persian name of the god Baga. So also the name Bigtha (Esth. 1:10) comes from the same root. Haman, being promoted to the high position of vizier, had to be saluted very reverently, as second to the king, to whom almost divine honor was given.

2-4 The king's servants bowed low and did obeisance to Haman—all except Mordecai. The reason for Mordecai's refusal is not clearly stated. The Greek Addition declares that Mordecai deemed that such great reverence was due to God alone. According to the explanation of Mordecai himself, which he had given to his companions, he did this because he was a Jew (v. 7).

So he was accused on religious grounds as well as on grounds of nationality.

5-6 The king's servants reported all this to Haman, who, proud of his high position, saw in Mordecai's behavior a personal insult. But it seems that he was too cunning or afraid to make it a matter of court intrigue. He preferred to hit Mordecai at the source of his pride and resistance as a Jew. Therefore he decided to destroy the whole Jewish people throughout the provinces of Persia.

7 Haman now proceeded with the execution of his plan in the twelfth year of the reign of Ahasuerus, in the first month, which had a name similar to that in Hebrew, "Nisan." It was the period of the New Year in Persia. One of the important activities connected with it was the drawing of lots (Pur), through which, following the Persian belief, the gods pronounced human destiny for the succeeding year. To that end the gods assembled in the "chamber of the lot" for their annual meeting under the chairmanship of the supreme god Marduk to decide by lot the destiny of mankind. The drawing of lots was done by Magis, or heathen priests, in a celebration which included sacrifices to appease the gods. Elsewhere in the OT there are traces of the belief that the lot can express the will of God, for example in the condemnation of Achan (Josh. 7:18) and again in the division of the promised land among the tribes of Israel (14:2).

The date for the execution of Haman's plan was fixed for the twelfth month of the year, called as in Hebrew Adar. This was no accident, for at the midpoint of the month the Persians celebrated a feast called Anahita. It would be easier then, he saw, to incite the multitudes to violence against the "infidels."

8-11 Haman had to obtain the assent of the king for his diabolical plan. He proceeded therefore with a certain diplomacy. He did not name the people; he only mentioned that they were scattered throughout the kingdom and had a different religion and followed different customs, which led them to disobey the orders of the king. Haman suggested that they should be destroyed, and the treasury of the king would benefit to the extent of ten thousand talents. The king, it seems, was pleased with the faithfulness and watchfulness of the vizier, and as a sign of his authority he gave Haman his signet ring to seal the decree. The king actually declined the offer of the money for himself, leaving it to Haman and to the people to disburse.

12-14 The king's secretaries edited the order and sent it to all the officers of the various provinces in their own language. The content of the edict is given in the MT: "to destroy, to slay, and to annihilate all Jews . . . [on] the thirteenth day of the twelfth month, . . . Adar, and to plunder their goods." In the LXX we have a longer version of the edict.

The attempted liquidation of minority groups, whether on racial or religious grounds, has happened all too frequently across the centuries. Cicero accuses King Mithridates VI of Pontus in 90 B.C. of killing in one day eighty thousand Romans. Both Jews and Christians suffered likewise at various times during the period of the Roman Empire. The Jewish communities in Europe have a long history of persecution, not least at the hands of so-called Christians, in the Middle Ages and later. Our own century has witnessed Adolf Hitler's attempt to "solve" the Jewish question. The ugly side of human nature has not changed with the passing of the years.

15 The edict became known in Susa and provoked great consternation—"the city of Susa was perplexed." But the king and Haman devoted themselves to drink in order to silence, perhaps, the last voice of conscience that exists even in natural man. By one masterly stroke the author stresses the ignominy of their deed against the background of a bewildered city which probably had Jewish residents.

CHAPTER 4

MORDECAI'S
COUNTERMEASURES
Esther 4:1-17

1-3   Being at the court Mordecai would learn immediately about
the dangerous edict. There was no time to lose, so he proceeded
to action. Even if the name of God is not explicitly mentioned in
the MT as it is in the LXX, the action of Mordecai is a typically
religious one: he rent his clothes and put on sackcloth and ashes.
Also he went into the midst of the city with a bitter cry to awake
the attention of righteous citizens, and especially that of his own
people. Nothing spreads so quickly as bad news. Thus the Jews
in all the provinces soon knew about the impending danger; consequently there was "fasting and weeping and lamenting." No
doubt they were appealing to God, though this is not expressly
stated. The LXX adds here the prayer of Mordecai, which is
cited in the JB after v. 17 but which could be placed here equally
well. The mourning had two main purposes, to implore the mercy
of God and to protest against the cruel edict.

Queen Esther was alarmed by the strange behavior of Mordecai. She sent him new clothes through a confidential messenger, for in his present state he could not enter the court of the
palace; but Mordecai refused to change his clothes. Instead he
sent to Esther, who would probably be secluded in her apart-
ments, the news about both evils, the edict and the sum of money
Haman ordered to be paid into the royal treasury. Mordecai
explained to Esther the desperate situation and insisted that as
soon as possible she should intervene before the king on behalf
of her people. According to the LXX he besought her "to call
upon God and to speak to the king to deliver us from death"
(v. 8).

10-11 However, Esther, who was usually obedient to her adopted father, was reluctant this time to follow his request. She explained to him through her trusty messenger Hathach that nobody might appear before the king under punishment of death, unless that person was specifically invited by the king. Esther herself had not been called into the king's presence now "these thirty days." Her long absence may indicate that she was not in the special favor of the king. It is possible, on the other hand, to understand Esther's reluctance to endanger her life by taking such a great risk, especially when she had no assurance of success. Not everyone is like Isaiah, ready to serve God immediately (Isa. 6:8). Even great prophets like Moses and Jeremiah had their moments of hesitation (Exod. 3:11 – 4:13; Jer. 1:6).

12-14 Mordecai was deeply dissatisfied and grieved with Esther's answer. Being at the court he probably knew about it already. But he recognized that intervention by this Jewish queen was the only possible solution and the Jews' last hope in their desperate situation. Consequently his retort was sharp — not as he would address a queen, but as he would speak to his own adopted daughter. In these verses he makes two appeals. First, he appeals to the fact that Esther's own future is bound up with that of her people. If the edict were to come into effect, then not even her royal status would save her. Then Mordecai appeals to Esther to recognize in her present situation the workings of Providence. For a Jewess to be the wife of a Persian emperor was an extremely dubious position in the light of Jewish law and custom. She must see herself as having been placed there by a Providence that planned to use her to protect her own people (cf. the Joseph story in Genesis).

These verses remind us, moreover, of Mordecai's dream, placed by the LXX at the beginning of our book. That dream provides a background, as it were, for Mordecai's impassioned plea. So his plea took a third form. Were Esther not able to rise to the occasion, he inferred, divine Providence would assuredly find another way to give "relief and deliverance . . . for the Jews from another quarter" (v. 14). In other words, God would never let his covenant with his people be frustrated. But meanwhile, had Providence not chosen Esther to be obedient and so to offer herself at this vital crisis in history?

15-17 By this time, however, Esther too had come to recognize
that there was no other way, though she knew how dangerous it
was. And so she pleaded for spiritual support. She asked permission to gather the Jews of Susa and to call upon them to fast
for three days; she as well as her maids would join them in the
fast. This fast was probably accompanied by prayers and sup-
plications, as suggested by the LXX. At this point the latter
includes "Esther's prayer." But here we note the justly famous
words of Esther: "Then I will go to the king, though it is against
the law; and if I perish, I perish" (v. 16). Mordecai, finally sat-
isfied, went off to execute Esther's instructions.

CHAPTER 5

ESTHER BEFORE THE KING
Esther 5:1-14

1-8 In this presentation of Esther's audience with the king we approach the climax of the story. In the MT the description of her audience is short and soberly stated. In the LXX it is more dramatically described, for when Esther comes in wearing her splendid royal attire, which both revealed and adorned her beauty, she suddenly faints. "But God changed the king's spirit to gentleness" (Addition D, v. 8); he hastens from the throne and lifts her up in his arms. Some see here an act that reflects the grace of God in whose hand is the heart of the king (Prov. 21:1); so it is by the grace of God that the king holds out his scepter, the top of which she touches with her fingers. The excavations of Marcel Auguste Dieulafoy at Susa have revealed a picture of a king sitting on the throne and holding a scepter, thus confirming the description here.

The king, we read, is very ready to fulfill Esther's request "even to the half of my kingdom" (v. 3). Is this promise the mark of legend, or is it just "polite eastern exaggeration"? But Esther does not use this opportunity to make her real request. Possibly she is not ready to do so. Possibly she is waiting till she can be sure that the king is in the right mood to listen to her request. Instead she invites the king and Haman to a dinner which she has prepared in honor of the king (v. 4). At the dinner the king asks Esther once again to make her petition, exhibiting the same magnanimous generosity as before. Esther, however, is not ready even yet to reveal her request; she asks only the favor that he and Haman come to another and more intimate dinner the next day, one which she herself would prepare for them. The tension of the story increases, but Esther keeps delaying her petition. Why does she do so? Is she lacking in courage, or does the author want us to understand the difficulty of the situation? Or does he see her as, perhaps unwittingly, serving the purposes of a Providence whose moment for action has not yet come?

HAMAN'S PRIDE AND CONSTERNATION

9-14   The author leaves aside for the moment the role of Esther and the fate of the Jewish people and directs our attention to the relations existing between Haman and Mordecai; these take up his interest until 8:2. Some commentators see here an independent story fused to the previous one. For we see Haman, full of pride, going out from the banquet with the queen and boasting about it before his wife Zeresh and before his friends. But one thing overshadows his happiness — this stubborn Mordecai who refuses to bow before him. Haman evidently has no knowledge of the relationship between Mordecai and the queen. But his wife finds a quick solution to his problem. In doing so she reminds us of the resourcefulness of Jezebel, King Ahab's wife, in the matter of Naboth's vineyard (1 Kgs. 21:7). "Let a gallows fifty cubits high be made, and in the morning tell the king to have Mordecai hanged," says Zeresh to Haman. The account records that the proud vizier readily accepted his wife's advice and gave orders to have the gallows constructed (Esth. 5:14). According to Prov. 16:18, "Pride goes before destruction."

In this way the author brings the story to a new climax. Esther has not yet told the king about the impending pogrom of the Jews, yet Mordecai is to be hanged the next day. Never indeed have things looked worse.

CHAPTER 6

THE SURPRISING CHANGE
OF ROLES
Esther 6:1-14

The picture changes again. We are in the king's palace that same
night. The king cannot sleep. The LXX (6:1) notes that it is the
LORD himself who interrupts the sleep of the monarch. We do
not find the reason stated just as explicitly in the Hebrew text.
Yet the impression we gain is that the author believes in the
guiding hand of God's providence. This is because seemingly
trivial facts — the sleeplessness of the king, the note he finds written in the royal chronicles, the early morning appearance of Haman in the court — all bring about a turn in the destiny of
mankind.

It is while reading his nation's chronicles that the king is reminded of the services of Mordecai, which had gone unrewarded.
So the king, under the sudden impulse to repair such an omission,
decides to do something about it. If there were only one of the
nobles to advise! But here Haman is at hand. So Haman is called
to give his expert advice on how to reward a man "whom the
king delights to honor." Haman, blinded by his pride, can think
of nobody else worthy of such an award but himself. Thus his
advice is that this man "be handed over to one of the king's most
noble princes," who would then clothe him in royal robes and
conduct him through the city, proclaiming, "Thus shall it be
done to the man whom the king delights to honor" (v. 9). We
can imagine Haman's dismay when he learns that this man is to
be Mordecai whom he hates, and that he himself is to be the
noble to conduct him. We see here then the irony of Providence
who humbles the proud. We are again reminded of Joseph's story
(Gen. 41:38-44), as well of such passages as 2 Sam. 12:1ff. and
Matt. 21:40ff.

129

Contrasts now follow one upon another. Mordecai returns to his place in the gate, as if nothing had happened, though in his heart he must have been shaken at having failed to see God's guiding hand. Haman comes home with a mournful face and tells his wife and friends what has happened. They too must have been shaken by the news, and could not fail to have perceived it as a bad omen for his future career. This is pointedly expressed in the words of Haman's wife, "If Mordecai, before whom you have begun to fall, is of the Jewish people, you will not prevail against him but will surely fall before him" (v. 13).

We note that while it is true that Mordecai has been honored he is not yet safe; neither is Esther, nor are the Jews. Yet Zeresh and Haman's friends foresee his further downfall. "While they were yet talking with him, . . ." Haman is taken in haste to the banquet of the queen. Events now follow fast upon each other.

CHAPTER 7

HAMAN UNMASKED AND EXECUTED
Esther 7:1-10

1-4 The situation opens in almost the same way as in ch. 5. The king and Haman come once again to Esther's feast. The king, who evidently senses that Esther has something important on her mind, repeats to her the same generous offer: "even to the half of my kingdom." This time, however, Esther seizes her opportunity to pour out her heart before the king and, to his great astonishment, begs for her life as well as for the life of her people. Thus by implication she reveals that she belongs to the Jewish people who are under threat of extermination. If it had been the case of their being merely sold into slavery (and here she refers to Haman's bribe), she would not have troubled the king; but what her prayer is connected with is, in fact, a matter of life and death.

5-8 "Who is he, and where is he?" asks the bewildered king. He seems to have forgotten about the decree; probably he had no idea that it concerned the Jews, nor realized that Esther herself was a Jew. So now we arrive at the climax of the story when Esther reveals that this evil man is . . . Haman. The news comes like a thunderbolt from a cloudless sky. The king is bewildered by the news and, burning with anger, goes out to the garden to cool off and think through the implications of the queen's statement. On his part, Haman is dumbfounded by this sudden stroke of ill fortune and falls at Esther's feet, imploring mercy. The king returns and finds Haman in this compromising position; his fury knows no end: "Will he even assault the queen?!" The king's wrath thus meant the death of Haman (cf. Prov. 16:14). And so they immediately "covered Haman's face"; such was the custom

131

with the Greeks and Romans when a person was condemned to death.

9-10 One of the eunuchs, Harbona, adds helpfully that Haman had already erected the gallows to hang Mordecai. This, of course, only adds oil to the fire. "Hang him on that" exclaims the king, and they obey at once, hanging Haman "on the gallows which he had prepared for Mordecai." We see here, then, the judgment of history, or rather the God of history: the wicked falls into the pit which he has dug for others (cf. Ps. 7:15).

CHAPTER 8

THE KING REPAIRS
HAMAN'S EVIL

Esther 8:1-17

1-2 "On that day . . ." when Haman was executed and his property requisitioned for the king's treasury, the king gave Haman's house to Esther in order to compensate for her unfortunate experience. Esther then introduced Mordecai to the king and explained her relationship to him. Thereupon the king appointed Mordecai to Haman's position, "and Esther set Mordecai over the house of Haman." Thus Mordecai became a vizier, one of the great princes who had the right to come before the king (cf. Esth. 1:14).

3-6 In spite of this, Mordecai apparently did not have the right to revoke the king's decree against the Jews. So here again the intervention of Esther was needed. Thus Esther "fell at the feet" of the Persian despot, following the eastern custom, and implored him that "the evil design" of Haman against the Jews might be averted. The king held out his golden scepter to her, whereupon Esther rose to her feet and explained the petition which was her real concern. She would not ask the revocation of the king's decree, which was "irrevocable" following the laws of the Medes and Persians; instead she asked that he make a new decree averting the "evil design" of that evil man.

7-8 Though Esther was now, no doubt, in the king's favor, he is depicted as showing some impatience, saying that he had already, as it were, fulfilled her petition. Indeed, he tells both Queen Esther and Mordecai, he had already given them Haman's house, and Haman himself had been executed. Yet the king also acknowledges that a royal edict cannot be revoked. And so it came about that he gave them authority to write in his name another edict counteracting the effects of the previous one.

9-14 The edict was prepared on the twenty-third day of the third month, called Sivan, two months and ten days after the first one (following the MT). But following the Greek version the edict was prepared on the twenty-third day of the *first* month, Nisan. Some commentators believe that the latter tradition is more acceptable, as an action taken without delay. The new edict was written in the same form as the previous one (cf. 3:2), yet with this difference, that the Jews would have the right to defend themselves and "to destroy, to slay, and to annihilate" any armed force which might attack them (v. 11). According to the LXX "their writing should counterbalance the former edict" and "in hour of trial they may defend themselves against those who attack them." The text stresses that the messengers had to go to all the provinces in haste "on swift horses" (v. 10). It is also noteworthy that while the first edict was written to every province in its own language, this time, thanks to Mordecai, it was also written to the Jews in their own script and language (v. 9). The author makes it clear also that the Jews were to act only in self-defense and, though given permission to plunder, did not do so (9:10, 15-16).

15-17 Mordecai left the king's palace in "royal robes," presented to him by the king in accordance with Mordecai's high position. The city of Susa rejoiced, not only the Jews therein but also all who had been perplexed by Haman's orders (3:15). "The Jews had light and gladness"; they also gained "honor" after the humiliation they had experienced. And in every city to which the edict reached there was "a feast and a holiday." These last words have a religious connotation also, for there is no doubt that the religious community offered thanksgiving to God for his wonderful salvation. And many of the Gentiles (Heb. *'amme ha-arets*) "declared themselves Jews," not merely through "fear" of reprisals but rather through "fear" of the God of Israel. The LXX adds "and were circumcised," meaning that they actually adopted the Jewish faith. These people must have regarded the events they had witnessed as the victory of the God of gods.

CHAPTER 9

THE GREAT DAY OF PURIM
Esther 9:1-32

1-10 When the decreed day, the thirteenth of Adar, eventuated, the expected triumph of the heathen was changed into a defeat. In the first eight chapters of our book the author's main concern had been to tell the story of a historical event as he believed it to have taken place, a story filled with drama and suspense; but from this point on the demands of law and cult outweigh any dramatic considerations. Content now in this supplement to record in barest outline, the author seeks to make two points: first, historical reasons, as he sees it, for observing Purim on two different dates (cf. vv. 11-19); and second, the steps whereby the events narrated above were commemorated and institutionalized in the Feast of Purim (vv. 20-32).

The author gives no indication as to what happened in the interval of the nine months (or eleven; see p. 134) after the publication of the second edict (8:9); but judging from 9:2 and 5, and especially from v. 16, we must conclude that Haman's letter had fanned flames of enmity against the Jews throughout the empire. Whether motivated by Haman's propaganda or by their own greed, some of the Jews' enemies were eagerly waiting for the appointed day to obtain an easy victory. They were, of course, rudely disappointed when that fateful day arrived, for they met with a strong defense by the Jews and suffered great losses. Undoubtedly some of the opponents were defeated even before they began their pogrom, becoming aware at once that the supposed victims were well organized for defense. But they also discovered that the Jews were favored by the officials, governors, and satraps of the provinces, who feared (and respected?) the new vizier Mordecai (v. 3). There were, however, battles. In Susa the Jews killed five hundred men in one day's slaughter, among them the

ten sons of Haman, who according to the decrees of oriental law
had to pay for their father's crimes.

11-19   It seems that the one-day slaughter did not put an end
to the troubles in Susa; Esther asked the king for permission to
continue the fight on the following day, and the king granted her
request. Some commentators consider Esther's action to be highly
vindictive. Others think that it was both practical and realistic
in light of the customs of those days and as a deterrent for the
future (cf. 1 Sam. 31:10).

Nothing is said about how many Jews fell, for the fighting was
in the first place in self-defense, in accordance with the permission granted at Esth. 8:11. But it is more than possible that the
numbers of slain were highly exaggerated. For instance, 9:16
notes that the number of the slain in the provinces was seventy-
five thousand, though the LXX records only fifteen thousand.

The author intends to stress that the Jews fought for their
deliverance and not for material gain (v. 16b). They remembered
possibly the wrath of God that fell upon King Saul for taking the
spoil of the Amalekites (1 Sam. 15). Other commentators suggest
that the author could have been inspired by a still older tradition,
that concerning Israel's ancestor Abraham. For Abraham took
no spoil in his battle against the kings of Canaan at the time
when he rescued his nephew Lot; it was in order that no one
might say, "I have made Abram rich" (Gen. 14:22-24).

The Jews in the provinces who fought on the thirteenth day
of Adar celebrated their feast on the fourteenth. But the Jews of
Susa, who also fought on the fourteenth, held their feast on the
fifteenth. It seems that the author is concerned to establish "historical" reasons for the dates of the feast. It is interesting also
that the Mishnah tractate *Megillah* (A.D. 250) fixes the dates for
the reading of the Esther scroll "in the walled cities" for the
fifteenth of Adar, but "in the villages and large towns" for the
fourteenth. Here then the story of the book of Esther really ends.

20-32   But how did Purim become established as a festival? The
author outlines here the three major steps whereby Purim, although not sanctioned in the Pentateuch (cf. Exod. 34:18-27),
became a festival and an element in the Jewish religious calendar.
The reasons given are: (1) Mordecai's festal letter (Esth. 9:20-22);

(2) the Jews' deliberate declaration of their intention to celebrate the feast annually in remembrance of their deliverance (vv. 23, 27-28); and (3) the second letter, written by "Queen Esther and Mordecai the Jew" (vv. 29-32), confirming the first one.

Yet some believe that the passage 9:20– 10:3 comes from an independent source, and that for a number of reasons. For example, the author refers to "the book of Chronicles of the kings of Media and Persia" for an additional account (10:2). Also, in 9:32 it is noted that Queen Esther's command was recorded in writing. And again, in a number of particulars 9:20– 10:3 contradicts the earlier account given in the book. According to 9:19 the Jews living in the "open towns" keep part of the fourteenth and part of the fifteenth of Adar as a feast, but in vv. 21-22 Mordecai recommends the keeping of both days as a feast. In v. 22 the sending of gifts to the poor is prescribed as a part of the observance of Purim, whereas v. 31 says that "fasts and lamenting" are also recommended. Some suggest that Purim could have its origin in a pagan feast (3:7), which only later became a feast of deliverance for the Jews. At 9:24-29 the author explains the reason for the name of the feast "Purim," that it comes from *pur*, i.e., "a lot," or the "lots" which Haman cast to destroy the Jewish people in Persia.

CONCLUSION

29-32   It seems that the first letter was not effective enough or had not reached all the Jews in the empire. Therefore the second letter went out to give "full written authority" to the first, stressing its title and the authority of its writers. It went from "Queen Esther . . . and Mordecai the Jew . . . to all the Jews, to the hundred and twenty-seven provinces of the kingdom . . . in words of peace and truth" (vv. 29-30).

The final words, "peace and truth" (Heb. *shalom we-emet*), bear a deeper meaning than the usual oriental greetings of "well-being and prosperity." They express wishes of peace and well-being to the community in both the material and the spiritual sense. Hebrew *emet* is used to confirm the faithfulness and integrity of their faith in the God who will not leave or forsake them; for God is *emet* —reliable, constant, faithful, and true.

The letter also contains a recommendation "that these days of Purim should be observed at their appointed seasons" (v. 31). Here for the first time fasting and lamenting in the sense of worship and prayer is recommended (cf. 4:3, 16). Apparently the fast originally took place in the month of Nisan (cf. 3:7), but later the three days of fasting were transferred to the month of Adar; Nisan was considered to be a month of rejoicing, for it recalled the erection of the tabernacle in the wilderness. At first the Jews fasted on three separate days (Monday, Thursday, Monday), but in the period of the Talmud (ca. A.D. 500) the fasting was limited to one day, the thirteenth of Adar.

CHAPTER 10

POSTSCRIPT
Esther 10:1-3

The book closes as it began, with praise of the greatness and might of Ahasuerus. Mordecai is remembered as "next in rank" to the king (even as Joseph had been).

The LXX concludes with another Addition, which gives the interpretation of Mordecai's dream, showing how all the great events were brought about by the providence of God. In earlier years God had raised up another Persian monarch, Cyrus, to perform for him the task of setting his people free from their long exile in Babylon. Isaiah 45:1 actually declares that God had addressed Cyrus as his anointed, or "messiah," but adds, "though you do not know me" (v. 5). So too God had used the greatness and might of Ahasuerus, even though his personal character was probably far from attractive. He too was "anointed" even though he "did not know the God of Israel," in that all unwittingly he acted in accordance with the providence of the God who had made covenant with Israel for the sake of all the peoples of the earth.

BIBLIOGRAPHY

Commentaries

Ellicott, C. J., ed. "The Book of Esther," in *A Bible Commentary for English Readers* (1905; repr. Grand Rapids: Zondervan, 1959) 3: 511-29.

Knight, G. A. F. *Esther – Song of Songs – Lamentations.* Torch Bible Commentary (London: SCM, 1955).

Moore, C. A. *Esther.* Anchor Bible (Garden City, N.Y.: Doubleday, 1971).

Paton, L. B. *The Book of Esther.* International Critical Commentary (Edinburgh: T. & T. Clark and New York: Scribners, 1908).

Ringgren, K. V. H. *Das Buch Esther.* Das Alte Testament Deutsch (Göttingen: Vandenhoeck & Ruprecht, 1958).

Other Works

Berg, S. B. *The Book of Esther: Motifs, Themes and Structure* (Missoula: Scholars Press, 1979).

Henshaw, T. *The Writings* (London: Allen & Unwin, 1963).

Hoschander, J. *The Book of Esther in the Light of History* (Philadelphia: Dropsie College, 1923).

Ironside, H. A. *Notes on the Books of Ezra, Nehemiah, and Esther* (New York: Loizeaux Brothers, 1951).

Moore, C. A. *Daniel, Esther and Jeremiah: The Additions.* Anchor Bible (Garden City, N.Y.: Doubleday, 1977).

Olmstead, A. T. *History of the Persian Empire* (Chicago and London: University of Chicago Press, 1948).

Roth, C. *A Short History of the Jewish People*, rev. ed. (London: East & West Library, 1959).